THE ECONOMY

Old Myths and New Realities

Walter W. Heller

W·W·Norton & Company·Inc.
New York

Library of Congress Cataloging in Publication Data
Heller, Walter W
  The economy.
  Bibliography: p.
  1. United States—Economic conditions—1971–
  2. United States—Economic policy—1971–
  I. Title.
  HC106.7.H44   1976   330.9′73′0925   76–21668
  ISBN 0–393–05595–7
  ISBN 0–393–09151–1 pbk.

First Edition
ISBN 0 393 05595 7 (Cloth Edition)
ISBN 0 393 09151 1 (Paper Edition)
1 2 3 4 5 6 7 8 9 0

Contents

Foreword

This book focuses on the economic problems of the mid-1970's, a period when economists, the economy, and economic policy have been under siege. In economic affairs, the unprecedented has become commonplace, to wit:

- a menacing double-digit inflation curbed but not cured either by our first "peacetime" price-wage controls or by the highest unemployment rates in 35 years;
- the longest and deepest recession since the Great Depression of the 1930's;
- an energy crisis that caught us unawares and hence unprepared and remains unresolved;
- startling jumps in the relative prices of farm prices and energy, the end of an era of cheap food and oil;
- the highest interest rates and the biggest budget deficits in U.S. history;
- the near bankruptcy of one of the world's great cities;
- in the international economy the acceptance of the unacceptable, namely, dollar devaluation, the dethroning of gold, and floating (though managed) exchange rates.

In short, what couldn't happen here, did. And the resulting changes in the character and intensity of the problems facing the economic policy maker and the economics profession were profound. Ironically, they forced a conservative Republican administration, against its will and intent, into the most active role in peacetime economic management (the critics would say mismanagement) that the country had yet seen. The grist for the mills of economic controversy and disagreement proved to be endless.

Part I grapples with the economic issues that an inflation-prone and unemployment-ridden economy casts up to the nation's policy makers. It is based in substantial part on articles written as a member of the *Wall Street Journal*'s Board of Economic contributors and on testimony prepared for Congressional committees in the past three years. And to provide a running account and more rounded perspective on the domestic economic problems that plagued the country in those unsettled years, I have supplied connective tissue, missing links (like the New York story), a series of charts for the times, and some thoughts for the future.

As Part I deals with the troubled economy, Part II deals with the troubled economist. For the economic events of the 1970's left their stigmata not just on the U.S. economy but on its economists. We had no surefooted theory of the new stagflation. And our forecasts of inflation went badly awry in 1973 and 1974. But beyond this, it was also charged that too much of the high-powered talent of the economics profession was devoting itself to solving puzzles for their own sake, to answering questions that no one had asked.

Running economics and economists down became a favorite sport of critics both inside and outside the profession. To contribute to a more balanced perspective in the face of this cascade of criticism—to help sort out what economists do and do not do well, in particular, what they can and do contribute to better policy making—I devoted my recent American Economic Association presidential address to "What's Right with Economics," an edited version of which constitutes Part II of this book.

Apart from more general observations on the role of economists and their areas of agreement and disagreement, Part II examines illustratively the specific uses of economics as an instrument for better policy-making in public finance and goes on to explore what economists have learned, and have yet to learn, about the inflationary process.

Acknowledgments

Apart from the acknowledgments to those who contributed so generously to the thinking in Part II, I want to pay a special tribute to my sounding board, my wife; to my secretary, Mrs. Sandra Mathisen, without whose unfailingly constructive, devoted, and cheerful help I would still be writing this book; and to Donald S. Lamm, whose uncanny ability to thread an editorial needle, separate wheat from chaff, and unmix metaphors has been an invaluable asset in producing this little volume.

THE ECONOMY

Part I

THE
TROUBLED
ECONOMY

THE 1970's HAVE BEEN YEARS OF TURBU-
lence for the economy—and for economists. Both unemployment and inflation jumped beyond the pale of
previous postwar experience, the experience from
which economists and policy makers had been taking
their cues. And to compound the confusion, the inflationary disease stubbornly refused to succumb to the
usual harsh treatment of recession, slack, and unemployment.

Instead, the combined rate of inflation and unemployment—the "discomfort index" or, to the economic policy

Chart 1. Inflation + Unemployment, 1954–76

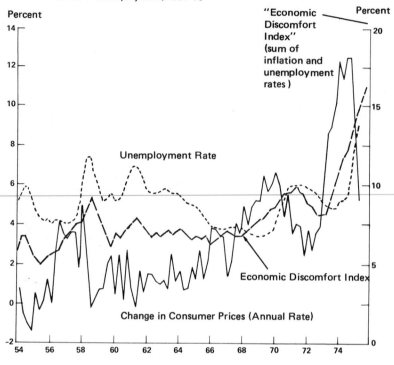

Source: Bureau of Labor Statistics.

Note: Price changes are percent changes in adjacent quarterly averages converted to annual rates. Unemployment rates are quarterly averages.

maker, the "discomfiture index"—climbed to new heights. As Chart 1 shows, the index that had moved within a range of 6 to 8 percent for the decade before 1969, shot up to nearly 20 percent in 1973–74 (before receding to a still-high 14 percent in early 1976).

At the same time, the economy was subjected to jolting external shocks like crop failures, the OPEC oil price explosion, and a series of twists, turns, and miscalculations in domestic economic policy that added to the atmosphere of economic uncertainty and doubt.

As brought out in Part II sudden changes in supply

conditions and prices of primary commodities also rudely forced their way into economic models and economic policy thinking—and helped make a shambles of inflation forecasts in 1973–74. Economic prophets will henceforth keep a warier eye on supply shifts—especially emerging scarcities and their price and purchasing power impacts—side-by-side with their traditional tracking of aggregate demand. Inflation forecasting will continue to focus on labor costs as a point of departure but will make ample room for changes in supply conditions, especially food, energy, and raw materials. A new awareness and a deeper sense of humility are not only becoming to the economic prognosticators and the policy makers who look to them for advice, but will also lead, in time, to better forecasts and better policy.

The following account covers perhaps the most difficult and demanding of the "years of turbulence." It begins in October of 1973, the month of the OPEC embargo that shocked us out of our energy complacency, and runs through the worst peacetime inflation in memory, the severest recession since the Great Depression, and on into an economic recovery beset by stubborn, if moderating, inflation and by continuing rates of unemployment and idle capacity known only at the troughs of previous recessions.

This is not to suggest that the winds of economic change were not blowing before the oil embargo. Even during the record eight years of uninterrupted expansion in the U.S. economy from 1961 to 1969—which began with four years of virtual price stability—the inflationary cat was let out of the bag when the costs of Vietnam were not matched by tax increases. And when the recession of 1969–70 failed to rebag the inflationary cat—even when the unemployment rate nearly doubled from its low point of 3.3 percent at the end of 1968 (see Chart 1)—its paw prints were on the wall: excessive inflation in a stagnating economy, or "stagflation," would be a recurring, if not persistent, challenge to economic policy makers of the 1970's.

On August 15, 1971, President Nixon astonished the

world with his "New Economic Policy," an about-face on domestic and international economic policy that knows no parallel in modern American history. He had again and again denounced government wage and price controls, denied that he would abandon the gold standard or devalue the dollar, and decried tax cuts to pump up the economy. Yet, under the pressure of economic events in the summer of 1971—persistent inflation, a sputtering recovery, and a hemorrhaging flow of dollars overseas—not to mention the influence of the presidential election looming in 1972, he took precisely the steps he had so consistently condemned.

Given Nixon's deep distaste for interference in private economic affairs, his decision to freeze wages and prices for ninety days was the most startling part of his program. Never before in an economy on a peacetime footing (by 1971, military spending including Vietnam was roughly 7 percent of GNP) had the country applied direct and forcible wage-price controls. Yet, with widespread public support, the comprehensive freeze worked. It broke the stride of inflation.

After ninety days, the freeze, known as Phase 1, was supplanted by a hastily improvised Phase 2. Still mandatory and widespread in their application, the Phase 2 controls got off to a shaky start. But gradually by adopting workable standards of average price increases of "no more than 2½ percent per year" and pay increases of 5½ percent, and by focusing most of its enforcement efforts on big business and labor, Phase 2 gained a firm foothold. It was considered one of the most successful postwar experiences in curbing inflation through direct wage-price intervention.

Yet, early in January 1973—with the economy under a full head of steam in response to over-expansionary budgetary and monetary policies in 1972—Phase 2 was junked in favor of a semi-voluntary and haphazard Phase 3.

But that was not the end of the saga of on-again-off-again controls. As 1973 unfolded with its succession of inflationary surprises, the White House responded first with a quixotic new price freeze in June that served, poorly, as a prelude to a new set of mandatory controls, Phase 4, introduced in August. It was even tougher than Phase 2, especially in its rules for pass-through of cost increases to final prices (for example, only dollar-for-dollar pass-throughs, with no percentage mark-ups, were permitted). However, it also provided for staged decontrol, industry by industry.

Meanwhile, the steam began to go out of the 1973 boom. Yet, when the following article was written, the country had no idea that it was just one month away from the recession of 1973–75 and only days away from the shock of the OPEC oil embargo.

The U.S. Economy in Transition

THE WALL STREET JOURNAL *October 8, 1973*

As one undertakes a reappraisal of the U.S economic outlook and tries to translate today's "tone" into tomorrow's numbers, one is struck with the pervasiveness of change—of transition from boom to slack, of flux in domestic and international monetary policy, of drift in White House political economy.

In part, the changes go beyond the horizon of the next year or two. The shift from surplus to shortage in agriculture and energy, the readjustment of the balance between economic growth and the environment, the continuing trend away from a goods-oriented to a services-oriented economy—all carry profound implications for longer-term economic outlook and policy, implications that are in large part the victim of not-so-benign neglect in a Washington, preoccupied with other matters.

Even more strikingly, the major facets of the economy that bear on the near-term outlook seem to be afloat on the seas of change:

- Inflation is about to recede from the unbelievable to the unpalatable. Propelled by the upsweep of world food and commodity prices, by the Phase 3 fiasco, and by excess demand, U.S. prices have raced upward at a 10 percent annual rate at the consumer level and 25 percent at wholesale from January through August. Next year, inflation's main thrust will probably come from cost-push as productivity slackens and labor once again plays catch-up with the cost of living. A slowdown to perhaps 5 percent in the inflation rate is a reasonable anticipation. Inflation, then, is changing in both intensity and character.

- Overheated expansion is beginning to cool. The rate of real growth has already been cut in half since last winter (from 8 percent to 4 percent), and further slowdown is in prospect.

- A dramatic change in the dollar's position in the world is under way. Its prolonged plunge in world money markets, now arrested, has shifted U.S. currency from a position of chronic over-valuation to one of unaccustomed under-valuation. In this process—aided and abetted by several years in which U.S. prices and unit labor costs have risen less rapidly than those of its competitors—the U.S. trade balance is shifting from a $6.5 billion deficit last year to approximate balance this year and a solid surplus next year.

Interwoven with these changes in economic parameters are important shifts now under way in every major segment of economic policy.

MONETARY POLICY: Though it will take some time to sort out just "what the Fed meant" last month when it gingerly drew back from its adamant tight money stance, it seems clear that the turn in monetary policy is under way. True, the financial markets over-reacted, and the Federal Reserve may have to take some corrective steps. But there seems little reason to doubt that—in the face of a slowing economy, painfully high interest rates, a drastic drop in money supply growth and the leaching of mortgage funds out of savings institutions—the Fed has modestly changed course and will lead us down a sawtooth path toward interest rates at least moderately below their recent lofty peaks.

FISCAL POLICY: Budget stringency, combined with inflated revenues, is shifting the U.S. full-employment budget from a sizable deficit last year to a sizable surplus this year, i.e., from stimulus to restriction. In spite of the recent furor over further fiscal tightening touched off by the White House charade on tax increases, such a move had little political future and, this late in the boom, would have been a case of economic overkill. Indeed, if the economy falters in 1974 and the White House continues to starve social programs by veto and impoundment, it may well be that considerations of both economic policy and political advantage will shift the emphasis from tax increases to tax cuts during the coming year.

INTERNATIONAL MONETARY POLICY: After two and a half devaluations of the dollar, after the controversial experiment with a "clean float," after a retreat to a "dirty float" since then, . . . the world is still in transit from the tight moorings and fixed parities of Bretton Woods to the distant land of "stable but adjustable" exchange rates.

WAGE-PRICE POLICY: Whether Phase 4 succeeds or fails, and whether it represents a phase-out of controls or a transition to a milder type of wage-price guidance, still hangs in the balance. Launched from deep in the credibility gap opened up by Phase 3, and lacking a foundation of conviction or moral thrust in the White House, Phase 4 is handicapped from the start. Yet, as in the case of Phase 2, one must hope that it will firm up after a faltering start.

Whether the devoutly desired "soft landing" of the U.S. economy in 1974 is possible in the face of these strong cross-winds of economic change is still an open question. A year ago, we could safely dismiss any threat of recession over a 12-month horizon. Today we cannot.

Two primary forces—booming exports and rising business investment in plant, equipment, and inventories—are cushioning the economy's descent from its giddy growth rates of last winter.

On the other side of the ledger are a growing number of soft spots in the economy: Housing is the most obvious one, and consumer spending the most perplexing. Attitude surveys showing sharp declines in consumer confidence are not reassuring—though not decisive either. Spending on durable goods will slacken in response to the slump in home building and the impact of rising prices and energy shortages on auto sales in 1974. On the other hand, sharply rising prices for non-durables—especially as clothing and gasoline follow food up the spiral staircase of inflation—will keep total dollar outlays by consumers rising and will hold the saving rate at relatively low levels.

Out of those opposing forces will come a further slowdown in the growth rate during 1974, a rise in unemployment, and the first drop in corporate profits in four years. But the betting odds at this distance are still against a scenario in which the expected slowdown to a growth rate of 2 percent to 3 percent in the first half of 1974 would turn into an "official recession" during the second half.

The wild card in the 1974 outlook is the rate of inflation. Haunting policymakers is the specter of 1969–71, when inflation defied all the rules of economic gravity and ignored the downward pull of economic slowdown, slack and recession. If a renewed price-wage spiral again puts inflation into a self-propelling orbit, the prospects for the mid-1970s are bound to worsen.

Since the world is unlikely to get caught as short of food in 1974 as it did in 1973, price pressures from this quarter will be less intense. The drop in wholesale prices last month is a good omen. The runup in other commodity prices touched off by the world-wide boom should be behind us by next year as country after country cools off its overheated expansion.

But countering these favorable factors will be two adverse forces: first, a rise in costs of non-food consumer goods that has not yet worked its way through the pipeline and, second and more persistent, the basic cost-push pressure that will intensify as labor escalates its wage demands while lower expansion of output stunts the growth in labor productivity.

On the first point it is worth noting that while most of the surge in wholesale food prices has worked its way through to consumers, this is far from the case in consumer goods other than food. Only half of the 10 percent increase in wholesale prices of such goods from January to August has been passed through to the consumer level. So consumers still face a long hard winter of inflation in non-food commodities (which constitute 40 percent of the Consumer Price Index, as against 22½ percent for food and 37½ percent for services).

On the second point, the intensity of cost-push pressures in 1974 will vary with the effectiveness of Phase 4, with the rate of wage escalation, and with the rate of growth in output. Given the unknowns regarding each of these forces, let alone the interactions among them, it is hardly surprising that appraisals of the course of unit labor costs in 1974 bristle with uncertainty.

The critical policy link in this chain is Phase 4. Will it work? How long will it last?

That it operates under severe handicaps is clear enough for all to see. Given the ruins of Phase 3 and Freeze 2 as its launching pad, given the back of Mr. Nixon's hand at its birth and little attention since, and given a choking burden of undigested cost increases to pass through to consumer prices during its infancy, Phase 4 might seem doomed to futility and an early demise. In the face of these handicaps—not to mention the growing public disenchantment with controls that grows out of them—how can one retain any hope that Phase 4 will follow the pattern of Phase 2 in moving from a wobbly start to a useful existence?

The answer lies in part in the toughness and realism of the main architect and manager of Phase 4, John Dunlop. Further, one can quarrel with the coverage of Phase 4 and criticize its complexities, but its central rules and framework—especially the lodging of both price and wage control in a single agency—provide a reasonable basis for meaningful price-wage restraint.

But is there the will to make it work? So far, very little of it is evident in the White House. A President otherwise occupied and sharing a natural distaste for controls with his chief economic advisers has limited himself very largely to *ad hoc* intervention in response to political pressures. Against the reportedly unanimous advice of his economic experts, he sprang his Freeze 2 surprise. In response to a wave of gasoline station closings, Mr. Nixon undercut his Cost of Living Council by prescribing early action to provide price relief. And if the council is looking for moral support in the form of White House briefings and appeals (à la Johnson) to business, financial and labor groups or televised calls (à la Kennedy) for public understanding and cooperation, it will apparently look in vain.

Yet, with 89 percent of the public putting inflation at or near the top of their list of concerns in a recent Gallup Poll (while only 14 percent listed Watergate) and with the anti-inflation battle far from won, there's enough at stake to give Mr. Nixon pause in any early move to gut or junk Phase 4.

- How can the sagging confidence of consumers, who could readily turn the 1974 slowdown into the second Nixon recession, be restored unless there's some assurance of success in the battle to check inflation?
- If controls are phased out too soon, what assurance remains that the slowdown generated by tough fiscal and monetary policies will be translated into slower inflation?
- If inflation is not reigned in, won't this be an open invitation to the Fed to reverse its move toward ease—and with it, reverse the odds against a recession?
- How could Mr. Nixon count on labor to continue its remarkable wage moderation unless there are prompt and persuasive signs of price moderation? Forestalling a repetition of the vicious price-wage spiral that wrecked

White House economic game plans and racked the country's economy from 1962 to 1971 is the most compelling single argument against too early a phaseout from controls.

Hopes for holding wage escalation within manageable limits rests in considerable part on the new look in the bargaining processes in the steel, aluminum and can industries. Not only has their bargaining timetable been moved up sharply, but if their negotiations reach an impasse, unions and management have agreed to submit their final offers to binding arbitration early in 1974. If inflation shows convincing signs of ebbing and if, in addition, the wage-wage sequence—the precedent set by recent major wage settlements—plays a major role in setting the unions' sights, these pattern-setting settlements will weigh in at a 7 percent or 8 percent rate of increase rather than the 10 percent to 12 percent advances that were common the last time around. Such a result would be stability-eroding, but not stability-exploding, and it would occur well before April 30.

Given the interplay of political and economic forces, it may turn out that the broad mandatory controls of Phase 4 are not so very long for this world (if "long" means more than seven months). One has to hope that Mr. Nixon's decisions will be based, not on the cold calculus of politics, but on the careful calculation of the economic risks. The consumer does not want to be left out in the cold again by another abrupt move toward decontrol.

Rather, the ideal course would be a carefully programmed pruning-out of those parts of Phase 4 that either can't work or shouldn't work, or both. For example, in the absence of export controls, and in the presence of high and rising prices in world markets, controls on beef and fertilizer will both distort and shrink the supply for domestic uses. And one can rely on competitive forces to hold prices in check in most retail areas, with this proviso: that effective controls are retained to curb the mark-ups by producers who have enough market power and discretion to set prices above the point at which demand and supply would intersect in a free market. In short, a gradual move toward milder controls of much narrower scope looks like the course of wisdom in 1974.

On balance, it seems unlikely that the bad luck and mismanagement that generated run-away prices in 1973 will be repeated in 1974. It takes faith in both natural forces and man-made policies to project a sufficient ebbing of inflation in 1974 to prevent a crippling new price-wage spiral and the consequent break-over of economic softening into economic recession. Yet, barring unforeseen acts of God and man, the foregoing exercise in political economy leads to this hopeful conclusion.

"Unforeseen acts of God and man" were, alas, in the making. The explosion of oil prices and the second successive year of crop failures were to knock 1974 inflation forecasts almost as far awry as 1973 forecasts. The following article correctly identified the components of the problem and the sources of possible surprises, but failed to foresee the continued run of bad luck, of external shocks that would escalate inflation well into the double-digit range in 1974.

Inflation, with All Cards Wild

THE WALL STREET JOURNAL *November 14, 1973*

The closer one looks, the worse it looks. The shadow cast by the oil crunch is darkening the inflation outlook for 1974. Oil is just the latest—and perhaps the most treacherous—of the villains in the drama of inflation forecasts gone wrong.

Time was when inflation forecasting was relatively straightforward: Project demand conditions and unit labor costs, make marginal adjustments for unusual developments in food or other commodity prices, and crank out the answer. Except for wars, tolerably good inflation forecasts resulted.

But the '70s have been a period of rude awakening for inflation forecasters. Defying economic slowdown and slack in 1969–71, inflation took off in a self-propelling spiral. Price forecasts had to make room for the forces of the wage-wage spiral and of self-fulfilling expectations. Beginning in 1971, the twists and turns of wage-price controls added another dimension of uncertainty.

But it is 1973 that will go down as the year of infamy in price forecasting. Never have so many been so wrong by so much. Prices raced ahead at twice the consensus forecast rate of 3½ percent to 4 percent inflation. Surprises were legion:

- Within ten days after the year began, the sudden dropping of Phase 2 controls in favor of the ineffectual voluntarism of Phase 3 knocked out an important prop of the moderate-inflation forecast.
- Next, the food price explosion took us unawares. While few forecasters accepted White House statements that food prices would be lower at the end of the year than at the beginning, none expected a 25 percent leap.
- Powered by a world-wide economic boom, the run-up in world commodity prices went beyond all expectations. The Reuters Commodity Index doubled within a year.
- Unforeseen dollar devaluations boosted import prices and contributed to shortages by stimulating exports.
- Indexes of industrial capacity (now revised) turned out to be deceptive. Demand-pull was upon us faster than we figured. (In a lonely but welcome compensating error, cost-push was muted by remarkable wage moderation.)
- The oil crisis, a late starter among the perils of price forecasting in 1973, is making up for lost time.

Conditioned by the turbulent experience of the past four years, the forecaster now goes well beyond the traditional demand-pull and labor-cost-push analysis to consider such factors as the state of expectations, the outlook for controls, the course of farm prices, the condition of world commodity markets, and the oil crunch. What are the portents for 1974?

DEMAND-PULL: Under the impact of restrictive monetary and fiscal policy, excess demand is ebbing. In measuring demand pressure, we have traditionally emphasized the degree of tightness of the labor market. This time around, limited plant capacity and materials shortages have loomed much larger and look considerably more stubborn. Some will evaporate as the boom subsides. But retarded expansion of industrial capacity in the past few years, short supplies of some primary products, and the energy crisis will plague us with more bottlenecks and their associated pockets of inflation than is usual in a softening economy.

LABOR COST-PUSH: As output gains recede and the rising cost of living is increasingly reflected in wages, the good performance of unit labor costs in 1971–73 will progressively erode. That the turn is already underway is suggested by the course of pay, productivity, and cost figures in the first three quarters of this year compared with the corresponding quarter a year earlier:

- The rise in compensation per man-hour has been steadily edging upward, from 7.3 percent in the first, to 7.4 percent in the second, and 7.7 percent in the third quarter.
- Productivity advances in the meanwhile have receded from 5.3 percent to 3.6 percent to 2.7 percent in the first three quarters.
- This combination has pushed the rise in unit labor costs from 1.9 percent in the first quarter to 3.6 percent in the second and 4.8 percent in the third.

With such steady advances occurring in a year of wage moderation, it's hardly surprising that the prospects of rising labor militancy and dwindling wage-price controls lead to apprehensions about 1974. If, in addition, the energy shortage superimposes sizable cutbacks in production on an already softening economy—as it seems destined to do—output per man-hour will falter, and unit labor costs will rise sharply. Part of this will impact on profits, but much of it will appear as cost-push inflation.

Will rising prices and rising costs chase each other up the spiral staircase of inflation as they did in 1969–70? In mid-1970 first-year wage-and-fringe increases in negotiated labor settlements exploded from 9 percent in the first quarter of 1969 to 16 percent.

Nothing this drastic seems in store for us in 1974. Neither the price-wage nor the wage-wage catch-up pressure is as intense as in 1969–70. And the new look in steel-aluminum-cans bargaining is on the side of moderation.

To be sure, labor will be a lot tougher in 1974 than in 1973. And cost-of-living escalators will fatten the recorded settlements. But starting from last quarter's averages of 7.8 percent for first-year increases and 6.4 percent per year over the life of the contract, wage escalation has a long way to go before its role in inflation shifts from erosion to explosion.

EXPECTATIONS AND CONTROLS: In part this conclusion depends on avoiding bad turns in the state of price expectations and the management of Phase 4 and its aftermath. If people have little hope that prices will ebb, they will project the prevailing rate of inflation into the future and strike their wage and price bargains at terms that protect them accordingly. That's how price-wage spirals are born. In the remaining months of its life Phase 4 has the difficult task of de-escalating not only price rises but price expectations and then giving way to a wage-price monitoring system that will help curb the post-controls flare-up in prices. Failure would invite a new self-propelling wage-price spiral.

FOOD PRICES: After the 25 percent jump in food prices during 1973, prices will be high. But with reasonable luck in next year's growing and harvesting weather, a further rise of as little as 4 percent from December to December looks like a good bet.

After the disaster of 1972 when world grain output dropped for the first time in a decade, farm output is back on the growth track in 1973. Both the U.S. and Russia are having good crop years. Farm and wholesale food prices are about 10 percent below their August peaks. Lower and less volatile grain prices are creating a more viable environment for expansion of broiler, hog, and cattle production.

As to processed foods, one major processor reports that net increases in raw material prices have been digested and that unabsorbed labor and transportation costs will add only 2 percent or 3 percent to final product prices. "In a growing number of cases, it's competition, not Phase 4, that's holding our prices in line."

According to the estimates of John Schnittker, the world will need to add 30 million tons to its grain output in 1974 to meet the average increase in demand. With the aid of extended acreage and the incentive of high prices, farmers are likely to meet this target, weather willing. But one should never leave the subject of farm prices without the caveat that, with demand up sharply and stockpiles down to wafer-thin levels, the world food situation is still close to the razor's edge.

OTHER COMMODITY PRICES: Echoes of the world's commodity price explosion in 1973 will still be heard in 1974, especially in the first half. Leaving aside oil for the moment, one finds that world spot prices of primary products rose nearly 30 percent in the first half of 1973 and, even with some easing in the current quarter, will have risen another 20 percent in the second half. As the world-wide economic boom subsides, spot prices should drop perhaps 15 percent to 20 percent during the coming year.

Actual transactions prices are not only much less volatile but lag well behind the spot price changes. Thus, even when spot prices recede, average import values of primary commodities will continue to rise for a time:

- In 1973, their rise was on the order of 15 percent in the first and 12 percent in the second half.

- In the offing for 1974 is a delayed-action rise of least another 5 percent in the first half before leveling off in the second.

Even with some price increases still in the pipeline, the easing of price pressures of primary products, excluding oil, will have a moderating influence on the rate of inflation in 1974.

THE OIL CRUNCH: The more deeply one probes the dark recesses of the oil and energy problems, the plainer it is that there are nothing but hard ways out. Even if King Faisal relents in a few weeks or months, the supply crunch, and especially the price crunch, won't.

Caught with its guard down, the White House is only now owning up to the severity of the energy shortage even aside from the Arabian embargo and the gravity of that crisis if the embargo continues. The oil sheik-down, coming on top of the rising cost of short supplies of U.S. energy, seriously imperils the 1974 inflation outlook. We need not wait for computer printouts to recognize the grim contours of the problem:

- Even before the sheiks posted their huge price increases and choked off supplies in October, the price index of "fuels and related products and power," representing 7 percent of the U.S. Wholesale Price Index, had risen 20 percent from September 1972 to September 1973. (Refined petroleum products rose 35 percent.)
- Given leaping crude oil prices and the tightening energy noose, a further price rise of 30 percent to 40 percent in the fuels category between September 1973 and September 1974 seems a reasonable conjecture.
- Since perhaps half of this price rise will pass through to the consumer level and since fuel and related items comprise about 6 percent of the CPI, one arrives at a rough approximation of a one percentage point increase in the cost of living in 1974 from the direct effects of the oil and energy crisis. Secondary effects, especially

through shortages in key petro-chemicals and plastics where inelastic demand can send prices zooming, could materially enlarge this impact.

- Finally, much depends on whether the White House follows its nose and depends largely on higher prices and taxes to allocate energy or holds its nose and resorts mainly to government controls and rationing. In the short term, the former approach would lead to considerably greater price rises.

The foregoing exercise leads to a forecast, excluding oil, of a 5 percent to 6 percent rate of increase in living costs in the first half, and 4 percent to 5 percent in the second half, of 1974 (with a somewhat slower rise in the GNP deflator). The energy shortage will add a percentage point or more to these numbers. But with so many unknowns still clouding the price picture, all forecasts of 1974 inflation, including this one, should be taken for what they are at the moment: subject to change without notice.

As the foregoing article was written, the impacts of the oil embargo and price escalation by OPEC countries were beginning to spread through the U.S. economy. Superimposed on the economic slowdown already underway as a result of the tightening of monetary and fiscal policies earlier in 1973, the oil crunch virtually assured a U.S. recession. Indeed, hitting most other industrial countries even harder, it touched off a worldwide recession.

The great sense of urgency generated by the embargo was matched only by the sense of confusion in the White House and Congress. Although a few economists and oil industry representatives had for several years warned that a day of reckoning on energy supplies was not far off and that the growing dependence on foreign oil could put us over a barrel, such warnings had triggered no useful contingency planning. The country was plainly floundering, the lines at the gasoline pumps were growing longer, and a sense of apprehension was mounting.

Small wonder that congressional committees "took to the hearings" in their bewilderment. Those of us who testified did our best to identify the short-run impacts on the economy and the long-run imperatives for a sensible national energy policy. One such undertaking was my testimony before a unit of the Joint Economic Committee in December 1973, excerpts from which follow.

Energy, the Economy, and Policy

STATEMENT BEFORE SUBCOMMITTEE ON
INTERNATIONAL ECONOMICS, JOINT ECONOMIC
COMMITTEE, U.S. CONGRESS *December 12, 1973*

Once again, in today's energy crisis, Americans are learning the costly lesson that we can't manage economic policy as if there were no tomorrow. But we seem to be slow learners.

Since the energy crisis abounds in unknowns and unknowables, in economic uncertainties and political indecision, one cannot proceed to an understandable economic appraisal without specifying certain critical assumptions.

Let me start with one central proposition for the longer run. In spite of Mr. Nixon's complacent assurances that the energy crisis is only "a temporary problem," and that "we will once again have those plentiful supplies of inexpensive energy," the Arab oil problem is here to stay. It is having essentially irreversible effects on U.S. energy prices and supply strategy.

First, the era of cheap oil and gasoline is rapidly slipping into history, never to return. The debate over whether we should cut gasoline use by higher prices, by higher taxes, or by rationing may have obscured the fact that petroleum prices are exploding all around us.

Second, in spite of Sheik Yamani's assurances that, once Israel withdraws to its pre-1967 borders, Saudi Arabia and its Arab oil cohorts would never again have any reason to embargo oil exports to the United States, we would be well-advised never again to treat Arab oil exports to us as anything but "interruptible service" energy. Even if the oil valves are not turned on and off for political reasons, we should never forget that the Oil Producing-Exporting Countries (OPEC) "oil-ogopoly" will henceforth manipulate its oil outflow—both up and down—to suit its profit and portfolio objectives. When it wants some more dollar assets, the valves will open. When oil in the ground looks relatively more attractive as a portfolio asset, the flow can be choked back or shut off.

It follows that our determination to develop alternative domestic sources of energy supply and cut wasteful uses and nonessential demand must not succumb to the euphoria of an eventual resumption of Arab oil flows. A credible and decisive commitment to develop our own fossil fuel capabilities and push ahead on more exotic energy sources will serve both our economic interests and those of our Arab-oil-dependent friends. Both our bargaining position on prices and our balance of payments will benefit. And our efforts to cut energy use and expand supply will pay off for Europe, Japan, and others in the form of both a more assured flow of Arabian oil and prices no longer supported by an unquenchable U.S. thirst for that same oil.

So I start with the basic assumption that high prices of energy are here to stay and that we cannot afford to turn off the drive for greater self-sufficiency when OPEC turns on the valves again.

In examining the impact of the energy crunch on the level of economic activity, one can usefully distinguish among several categories of negative effects on GNP, including

- cutbacks in consumer demand for things complementary to gasoline and other petroleum products (autos, tires, campers, motel services, meals away from home and so on) not offset by shifts of consumer spending to other goods and services;

- the direct loss of output growing out of reduced oil imports and the associated loss of value-added as a result of the slowdown in oil refining, distribution and the like;
- cutbacks in supply caused by bottlenecks in transportation, plant and office closings, and shortages of petroleum foodstocks for the petrochemical industry;
- temporary cutbacks in plant and equipment investment decisions because of hesitation, uncertainty and the process of shifting to less energy-intensive production.

By far the largest jolt to the economy will come from the demand side. A distinctly tentative assessment suggests a direct cut in consumer demand for things complementary to gasoline of nearly $15 billion at an annual rate during 1974. Some $7 to $8 billion of this drop would be in automobiles, brought about by a slump in unit sales to a range of 8 to 9 million (including 1.5 to 2 million imports) and a decided shift to small cars. Other demand complements associated with autos would account for much of the balance.

Although there would be sizable shifts in demand to other areas (one thinks of TV sets and other forms of home entertainment, coal, clothing and the like), there will be a period of confusion, anxiety, and hesitation that will lead to a higher rate of saving.

Even more important than the impact of the oil shortage as such is the impact of exploding prices. U.S. consumers will pay a "tax" of $15 to 20 billion in the form of higher prices for petroleum products in 1974. Those dollars won't be available to buy other goods and services.

The first half of 1974 will look like—and by traditional standards will be—a recession. We can expect a drop in real GNP at an annual rate of about one and one half percent in the first quarter and one percent in the second, followed by a moderate rise starting in the third quarter and a somewhat more rapid recovery in the fourth.

Given the foregoing projection of economic consequences of the oil shortages, one can expect a material worsening of inflation. As a function of the direct effects of petroleum price boosts and adverse effects on productivity—not to mention such ominous portents on the labor front as the reopening of the Teamsters contracts—an add-on of two to three percentage points to the advance in the cost of living for 1974 is in the cards. In other words, a rise of nine to ten percent in the first half of the year and six to seven percent in the second now seems in the cards. A rise of over seven percent in the GNP deflator during 1974 can also be expected.

Accompanying the drop in output will be a large and distressing jump in unemployment. It is likely to rise above 6 percent by the second half of the year.

I anticipate that the prospective jump in the rate of inflation triggered by the energy shortage will lead some observers to call on the Federal Reserve Board to keep its foot firmly on the monetary brake, primarily by cutting back the growth in money supply. But under present circumstances, such counsel would be misguided.

The extra price jolt from the oil shortage in 1974 should not be taken as a signal—any more than the 25 percent jump in food prices in 1973—for monetary tightening. These shortages, to use the words of Arthur Burns in his recent defense of monetary policy, "hardly represent either the basic trend in prices or the response of prices to previous monetary or fiscal policies." To attempt to hammer down price increases in food and oil—two sectors with flexible prices and inelastic demands—by restrictive monetary policy would wreak havoc on the rest of the economy.

Since an easier money stance was already in order before the cutoff of Persian Gulf oil, and since the major impact of that cutoff on GNP will come through discouragement of consumer spending, the Federal Reserve Board should definitely move in the direction of ease.

In so moving, it should use interest rates as its guide under present circumstances. The board should stop worrying about the demand-oriented increase in the money supply and concentrate on bringing short-term interest rates down to soften the impact of the energy shortage superimposed on an economic slowdown that was already in process.

In the field of fiscal policy, explicit steps are even more difficult to specify, but the general directions seem clear enough. The startling upsurge first in food and then in fuel prices (not to mention clothing) has been sharply regressive. Although food represents just about 20 percent of average consumer spending, this rises to 40 and 50 percent in the very low income groups. For the poor family that spends 40 percent of its disposable income on food, the 20–25 percent leap of food prices in 1973 represents a cut of 8–10 percent in real income. If we add to that a two to three percent cut via surging energy prices, the implication is clear: anything we do on the fiscal front in 1974 must, as a matter of equity, transfer funds to the lower income groups.

The case for tilting fiscal policy in this direction is reinforced by a consideration of the pattern of energy demand across income groups. The larger the family income, the larger the proportion that is likely to go for uses of energy that society would regard as nonessential or downright wasteful.

This does give us some clues to fiscal measures that might be appropriate. Especially to the extent that we increase excise taxes to curb gasoline use, we should make restitution to lower income groups via cutbacks in social security and income tax withholding and cash refunds to the poverty groups not covered by such withholding. Still within the framework of an energy tax, one should also consider providing free bus service or other commuter transportation for the lowest income groups.

But I do not mean to say that one has to stay within that framework to carry out the appropriate distributive objectives. In a period when events have cut deeply into the real incomes of poor families and when a great many unskilled and lower-income persons will be thrown out of work as a result of the energy crunch, it would make good economic and humanitarian sense to restore some of the cuts in social service budgets, expand the public employment program and eliminate payroll taxes on persons below the poverty line.

Turning to the energy field itself, I would not rely solely on the price mechanism, aided and abetted by tax hikes, to ration gasoline and effect the 25–30 percent cut that is vital to preserve the supply of petroleum required to sustain employment and output. Nor will the "do-it-yourself" or "catch-as-catch-can" system of rationing implied by the present system of allocations, combined with a squeezing down of refinery output of gasoline, do an acceptable job. It can only lead to long queues and mad scrambles at the gasoline pumps, grey-market payola, corrosive favoritism, tie-in sales and sweetheart deals at the service station—not to mention unwarranted profits.

For all its blemishes and administrative difficulties, an outright system of gasoline rationing remains the fairest, quickest and most acceptable way to go.

The choice of a particular form of rationing should be made on the basis of equity in distributing reduced gasoline supplies, minimizing black markets and counterfeiting and speed of putting the plan into effect. A system using negotiable ration coupons (distributed on a per-car or per-licensed-driver basis) or a basic ration plus high-premium coupons sold by the government could be quickly and simply put into effect. Or one could use citizen rationing boards as in World War II, except that everyone granted a special ration would get nontransferable stamps, say, red stamps, while the negotiable ones could appropriately be green. Once the rationing system were in effect, people would be free to use their ration as they pleased—without a detailed set of curbs on speed, car mileage, Sunday use and so on. Somewhat paradoxically then, rationing—especially if administered through the use of negotiable ration coupons—can be thought of as a way of preserving freedom of consumer choice.

To bulwark the rationing system, an increase of perhaps 10 cents a gallon in the gasoline tax would make good sense. Not only would it help cut consumption, but it would yield perhaps $8 billion a year that could be utilized in part for energy research and development, in part for mass transit and in part to finance payments and programs for lower income groups.

Finally, in summary form, let me list some other policy considerations and recommendations that bear on the alleviation of the energy shortage and the minimizing of its adverse impacts on the economy.

Using the levers of price controls and the authority granted by the Export Administration Act of 1969, the Administration should act to break specific bottlenecks like that in drilling pipe and tubular casing required for domestic oil exploration.

The hitherto unquestioned right of the Pentagon to commandeer oil for military use should be subjected to intense questioning, and its plans for military conservation of energy should be subjected to rigorous review by the new Federal Energy Administration.

The production of enriched uranium should be cut back in order to place at the disposal of other consumers as much as possible of the three percent of total U.S. electricity consumption that is used in this process.

Income tax subsidies for the oil and gas industries need to be changed in at least two ways, first, by requiring that funds freed by percentage tax depletion and related tax preferences be plowed into capital investment in the domestic oil industry and, second, that mineral depletion allowances and tax credits for royalties on Middle East ventures (perhaps on all overseas ventures) be ended.

We need to develop a more rational policy of leasing our own vast public resources of oil and gas (especially on the continental shelf) by reducing the front-end risks involved in the present leasing system and by providing for a sizable government share (perhaps 50–60 percent) in the oil and gas proceeds from operations on public lands or water.

The pricing structure for natural gas should be changed, first, by boosting rates to commercial and industrial users, second, by adjusting the ceilings on existing sources of supply and, third, by removing them on new sources (at least on private lands).

On electricity rates, we need to recognize that, in a global sense, electricity is an increasing-cost good. This calls for an end to quantity discounts and, indeed, rising rates on excessive consumption.

In other words, we should be using price, profit and tax incentives in a carefully guided way to protect the public and achieve national objectives.

As a final point, let me simply quote from a *Business Week* editorial of Dec. 7, 1973: "A multipronged approach to the energy problem is probably the right one. What the public needs to know is just what the prongs will be and how sharp. The unnerving thing about the present situation is the suspicion that the United States is blundering ahead with no real energy plan—simply hoping for the best."

The energy crisis gave rise to a bewildering array of schemes designed to curb the American appetite for energy—especially in the form of petroleum products— or to stimulate energy production, or both. Some offered quick fixes; others, long-range programs. Some relied on market pricing incentives, others on direct regulation.

Several months before the Arabs trained their oil weapon on the industrialized nations, a number of economists were stirring uneasily about the "energy squeeze" and offering proposals to cope with it. In mid-1973, I had occasion to raise a question that remains unanswered (in 1976) in spite of several White House and congressional skirmishes with the idea: Why not step up the gasoline tax—and impose companion taxes on other petroleum products—to ease the squeeze? In the following excerpts from my June 1973 article in *The Wall Street Journal*, "A New Role for the Gasoline

Tax?", I deal with the potential attractions of this approach to curbing the use of petroleum products.

A New Role for the Gasoline Tax?

THE WALL STREET JOURNAL *June 8, 1973*

Conserve energy, combat pollution, cut balance-of-payments deficits, curb inflation? Is the gasoline tax, that old workhorse of highway finance, about to become the thoroughbred Secretariat of the fiscal world?

How well would a boost in the present four-cents-a-gallon federal tax on motor fuels serve these new and glamorous purposes? Would some other tax device, say, a graduated auto excise tax, do a better job?

It is not easy to break out of our long-accustomed mold of thinking about the gas tax as strictly a highway user tax earmarked to pay for the benefits received or costs occasioned through our use of the highways. If we now blow its cover as a payment for highway services rendered, how are we to judge this tax? Here, the economist has a handy aid to clear thinking. Judge it, as we do other general revenue taxes, by its effects on income distribution, economic stabilization, and resource allocation, to wit:

- Distribution: Does it distribute tax burdens in a fair and equitable way?
- Stabilization: In the present context, will it contribute to economic stability by easing inflationary pressures?
- Allocation: Will it change the pattern or structure of resource use in a desirable way? Significantly?

Distribution. Studies show that the motor fuel tax, taking into account the approximate 50–50 split between private and business use, is moderately regressive—about the same as the beer tax, but considerably less so than the cigarette and local telephone taxes. In addition, like all selective excise taxes, the gas tax penalizes those who, perforce or by preference, spend a higher-than-average portion of their income on highway transportation. On these counts, the individual income tax, which takes account of the size of income and family obligations and does not discriminate among taxpayers according to their spending patterns, is obviously superior.

Stabilization. The portion of the motor fuel tax that bears on passenger transportation is effective in siphoning income out of the pockets of middle and lower income groups, and therefore offers some help in curbing demand.

But surely, proponents of the gas tax boost would be ill-advised to rest their case in any significant way on its anti-inflationary impact:

- Speedy passage is not in the cards if the highway lobby, pursuing its self-interest, makes common cause with liberals who rightly detest regressive taxes. Prolonged delay could bring the tax into effect just when the widely predicted slowdown of the economy takes hold.
- To the extent that the tax is a business cost (nearly 50 percent) or absorbs profits, it is not very effective as an anti-inflation device.
- Looking beyond its impact on demand-pull inflation, one finds an uncomfortable cost-push effect. Since gasoline represents almost 3 percent of the cost-of-living index, each five-cent increase would boost the index by 0.37 percent.

Allocation. Since the gasoline tax gets negative or mixed notices on equity and anti-inflation grounds, its claim to a new place in the fiscal sun must rest on its potential for cutting energy use and curbing pollution and congestion, that is, on its ability to divert resources to other and better uses. If it can significantly cut auto and truck use, spur gas-saving practices, and speed the shift to compacts and subcompacts, it can eventually accomplish through the market system much of what may otherwise require mandatory controls.

Once the gasoline tax is thus liberated from its highway-finance bondage, new fiscal vistas open up all around us:

- Why not couple with a gas tax increase a steeply graduated excise tax on new cars for the longer run? Graduation by gas mileage would be one possibility. Another would be graduation by weight—for example, running from 10 cents a pound for small cars to 20 cents for the heavyweight gas guzzlers. Either approach, while effective only on new cars, would accelerate the transition to light-weight cars.
- If curbing energy use is the object, why stop with gasoline? Aren't there other non-highway uses of petroleum that are also candidates for curtailment?
- For that matter, why stop with petroleum products? A graduated tax on natural gas with low rates on residential users, medium rates on commercial users, and high rates on industrial users might have some merit.

But let's not delude ourselves. If we travel the tax route to energy conservation and pollution control, it will be hard to take the regressive sting out of such taxes. Yet it must be done unless we are to ride past the energy crisis on the backs of the poor and near-poor.

The use of such taxes would, therefore, have to be accompanied by such moves as the following:

- Exercise of great ingenuity in constructing such taxes, whether through graduated rates, as in the case of the suggested auto excise tax, or perhaps by building in tax credits to shield the poor.
- Use of the proceeds to strengthen social and welfare programs for the lower income groups, whether in the form of services, income support, or voucher systems.
- Or if compensating action in the tax field is preferred, make the $80 billion-a-year social security payroll tax less regressive by exempting poverty-level wages, allowing for family size, and removing the upper limit on the wage base.

Using taxes to reallocate resources into energy-conserving and pollution-free uses via market incentives rather than government regulation is an alluring game. But the more vigorously we play it, the more important it will be to keep the distributive effects of such taxes front and center.

In mid-1973, when the foregoing article was written, studies of available data on gasoline indicated a rather high price elasticity of demand—a substantial response of consumers to a change in price. Using both cross-section and time-series data, studies showed a short-run price elasticity of -0.2 to -0.4 and long-run elasticities between -0.5 and -0.7. At the lower end, these numbers said simply that for every 10 percent increase in the price of gasoline, demand would shrink by 2 percent in the short run and 5 percent in the long run.

As more pertinent and reliable data were generated by the rapid run-up in the prices of gasoline, which almost doubled between 1973 and 1975, elasticity estimates were drastically revised downward—to only half the low-end numbers. A study by Data Resources Incorporated in early 1976 showed an "immediate" (one quarter) price elasticity of $-.07$. For the "short-run" (one year), as driving habits respond and budgets are readjusted, the elasticity rises to $-.11$. For the "long-run" (two to three years), as consumers shift to smaller cars and gas saving habits become more ingrained, the elasticity rises to $-.25$.

Given the long-run elasticity of $-.25$, a tax boost of 30 cents per gallon—that is, roughly a 50 percent increase in the average 1976 price of gasoline—would induce a cutback of 12½ percent in gasoline consumption. Translated into oil-equivalents, this would be a saving of 315 million barrels of oil a year, or about 5 percent of the 6.5 billion barrels the U.S. consumes each year—not inconsequential, but not staggering either.

The price responses of industrial users of petroleum products are much greater. Through re-engineering and direct cutbacks in unnecessary energy use in response to careful cost calculations, industry has already made impressive savings in energy. The possibility of stimulating further savings by excise taxes is worth further study.

Nevertheless, the new and more reliable elasticity data weaken the case for gasoline taxes as a conservation measure. Indeed, they also weaken the argument that reliance on the price mechanism in the case of gasoline—within price ranges now conceivable—will effect large energy savings. And the European experience with prices double or more the U.S. prices seems to corroborate this. In any future oil crunch, the case for distasteful direct measures like rationing is correspondingly strengthened.

The Softening Economy and a Hardening Budget

Although economic softness, with an extra push from the oil crisis, had already turned into the early stages of the 1973–75 recession, the Nixon Administration continued to fight a one-front economic war against inflation.

A number of economists, recognizing that recession was underway and that tough fiscal and monetary policies would do little to tame a food and fuel price inflation, urged measures to shield the economy against the cold winds of recession. For example, in an article for *The Wall Street Journal* of January 8, 1974, I stated:

> Given a proper response to the energy crunch, the economy's key problem as 1974 wears on will be a shortage of demand, not of fuel. And the Administration has an unusual opportunity to cope with that problem in ways that will couple sound fiscal policy with generous social policy.
>
> Last year, one could simultaneously applaud the Administration's fiscal policy—its swing from a full-employment deficit toward full-employment balance in the context of an overheated economy—while deploring its social policy—its choice of merciless slashes in social services over tax increases to fight inflation.
>
> This year, at a time when price and job developments have conspired against the poor, recession clearly calls for an ex-

pansionary budget [stressing outlays and tax cuts for the poor and near-poor].

The softening of the economy can best be seen in Chart 2, showing the gap between actual and potential GNP. (For an explanation of the concepts and calculations, see the "Special Note" accompanying the chart.) The long sustained expansion of the 1960's carried GNP back to its potential—indeed, above it when the economy overheated after escalation of the Vietnam War. Then after the economy had lost ground in the 1969–70 recession, the recovery in 1971–73 brought GNP back close to its potential. In late 1973 and early 1974, total output was already dropping rather markedly from the rising potential of the economy.

But in such passages as the following, the President's Budget and Economic Messages in February made crystal clear that the fight against inflation was to be pressed, recession or no:

- "We must dedicate ourselves to carrying on the fight against inflation in 1974 and thereafter."
- "Some slowdown in the growth in demand is appropriate to check inflation."
- "Therefore, I propose a budget which will continue a posture of moderate restraint. . . ."

As his measure of budget restraint, Mr. Nixon appropriately used the "full-employment budget," which relates expenditures to tax receipts in terms of a steady level of unemployment—4 percent was the standard used in the Nixon, Johnson, and Kennedy Administrations—and thus identifies changes in fiscal *policy* and sorts them out from the changes in the level of economic *activity* that are reflected in the actual budget. On the full-employment basis, Mr. Nixon projected a rise in the surplus from $4 billion in fiscal 1974 to $8 billion in fiscal 1975.

As it eventually turned out, the budget tightened much more sharply than this. Even while taxpayers' *real* in-

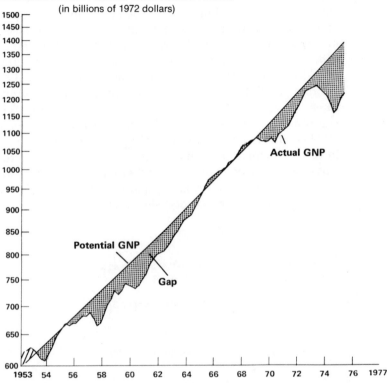

Chart 2. Actual and Potential Gross National Product
(in billions of 1972 dollars)

Special Note: Potential GNP purports to measure what the economy
would produce if all of its resources were fully utilized given the technology and institutional arrangements that have existed at the time. "Fully
utilized" has never meant the kind of utilization that would prevail under
wartime conditions but rather the utilization that could be expected under conditions of reasonable price stability. This has always been less than
complete utilization. Under ordinary circumstances, some unemployment
is present because some workers are in the process of changing jobs; similarly, some old plants are idle because market conditions do not permit
them to operate profitably. In the past, this degree of utilization has been
reflected in an overall unemployment rate of 4 percent. The rate of inflation associated with that degree of unemployment has typically not been
specified. Furthermore, notions of what constitutes reasonable price
stability can vary over time. (Prepared by the Council of Economic Advisers)

45

comes were falling, inflation kept boosting *money* incomes. Since federal taxes are levied on money incomes—and at progressive rates at that—the effective rates of federal taxes rose while real incomes fell. Thus, double-digit inflation snuffed out the usual automatic cushioning effect of a shrinking federal tax take during recession periods.

From a $5 billion full-employment deficit (at annual rates) in early 1973, the budget shifted steadily and sharply to a $32 billion surplus by the third quarter of 1974—a drastically restrictive swing. In contrast, as shown in Chart 3 (which presents the full-employment and actual surpluses as a percentage of full-employment GNP), the budget had shifted toward expansion in the 1957–58, 1960–61, and 1969–70 recessions. The 1973–74 case is unique.

Chart 3. Full Employment and Actual Budget Surplus as a Percentage of Full-Employment GNP, 1956–76 *

Budget surplus as a percentage of full-employment GNP

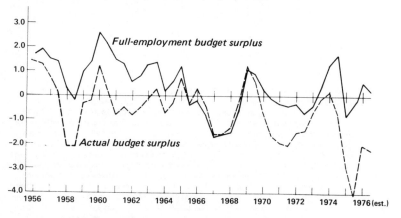

*Full employment implies an unemployment rate of 4 percent.

Source: B.M. Blechman, E.M. Gramlich & R.W. Hartman, Setting National Priorities, The 1976 Budget, Brookings, Washington, 1975, p. 32.

Meanwhile, the Federal Reserve System, after several months of monetary easing in response to the economic slowdown, abruptly reversed course in February 1974. Business loans had exploded, primarily to finance a pell-mell rush to build up inventories (thus aggravating shortages). The Federal Reserve authorities moved in with a vengeance. Money was tightened and interest rates moved back into double-digit range and remained there for many months as Chairman Arthur Burns and his associates held steadfastly to their restrictive course in the face of a continued weakening of the economy.

This, then, was the emerging economic scene and policy backdrop for the article which follows. Even though the odds in March still favored an economic upturn in the second half of 1974, such an upturn depended in part on a shift from fiscal restraint to fiscal stimulus.

The Case for Fiscal Stimulus

THE WALL STREET JOURNAL *March 11, 1974*

Once again, the battle between anti-recessionists and anti-inflationists is joined. Without differing very much on the projected 1974 economic scenario—downturn and double-digit inflation in the first half followed by an upturn and some ebbing of inflationary pressures in the second— the antagonists run the gamut from "ease up" to "hold tight" in their prescriptions for fiscal-monetary policy in 1974.

Part of this division reflects conflicting diagnoses of the nature of this year's recession and inflation. Partly, it grows out of divergent appraisals of how much of any given demand stimulus will translate into jobs and output and how much into more inflation (either now or later). And in no small part, it goes beyond positive economics to a conflict of values.

Nothing throws the issues into bolder relief than the

proposal for a quick income tax cut in the form of an increase in personal exemptions. A tax reduction of $5 to $6 billion a year could be effected either by boosting the per capita exemption from $750 to $900 or by adopting Senator Mondale's proposal to give the taxpayer the option of taking a $200 credit against tax or continuing to deduct $750 from income.

The equity case for this move is obvious:

- Before the year is out, inflation will have eroded the real value of the $750 exemption by more than 20 percent since it went into effect at the beginning of 1972.
- Even more important, boosting exemptions would concentrate the bulk of the tax benefits at the middle and lower end of the income scale where recent inflation, especially in the form of surging food and fuel prices, has exacted a particularly heavy toll. (To reach the lowest incomes calls for further action, e.g., a step-up in social service programs and relief from social security payroll taxes on the poor.)

Indeed, the social rationale for income and payroll tax relief in the lower brackets is so compelling that it would make sense even if it were matched by simultaneous tax increases elsewhere.

But equity aside, can a broad-based income tax cut stand on its *economic* merits? Those who say it can't—Messrs. Shultz, Burns, Fellner, McCracken, and Stein somehow come to mind—cite such arguments as these:

- Our current economic downturn is mainly the result of supply restraints, of shortages and bottlenecks. Such demand deficiencies as exist will soon correct themselves.
- Any further stimulus will simply increase the ferocity and tenacity of inflation.
- Mr. Nixon's fiscal 1975 Budget already contains all the stimulus the economy can stand. And besides, cutting income taxes today robs us of vital revenue-raising power we need for tomorrow.

Straw men? Hardly. But neither are they Holy Writ. First, as to the nature of recession. Though supply shortages get the headlines, a close look reveals unmistakable signs of a shortage of demand. The weary consumer, whiplashed by tight money and fiscal restraint and whipsawed by runaway food and fuel prices, has pulled in his horns:

- For nearly a year, his consumption of durables other than autos has fallen in real terms, while his consumption of nondurables and services has kept only a trifle ahead of inflation.
- As to autos, the gasoline shortage has converted an expected decline into an actual disaster. Lying behind the 27 percent drop in overall sales of domestic cars last month is a plunge of nearly 50 percent in demand for standard and larger models.
- Tight money has cut the rate of residential construction outlays from $60 billion a year ago to around $47 billion today.

For consumers, January was perhaps the cruelest month. While personal income dropped $4 billion, consumer prices raced upward at a 12 percent annual rate. Real spendable earnings of nonfarm workers, after taxes, were down 4 percent from a year earlier—the largest drop in ten years.

Nor is any early rebound in sight. It will be months before exploding oil prices have worked their way through the economy, soaking up $15–20 billion of consumer purchasing power in the process. For that's the amount of tribute the American consumer has to pay foreign and domestic producers of oil—and in the short run, very little of the funds thus siphoned off will reappear in the economy as demand for exports or increased dividends and capital spending by the U.S. oil industry. So even with an end to the Arab embargo, the U.S. economy will continue to suffer the paradox of "oil drag"—a cost inflation of prices and a tax-like deflation of demand.

A roll-back in domestic crude oil prices could materially

ease that drag. For example, a cutback in new oil prices to $8 and oil prices to $4.25, while maintaining strong incentives for boosting output of new oil and oil substitutes, would serve to cut oil-cost inflation by $5 billion; restore $5 billion of real purchasing power to consumers; stop that amount of excess profits at the source.

It isn't often that a single measure promises to cut cost inflation, bolster aggregate demand, curb profiteering, and still maintain vital incentives. Yet, doctrinaire pursuit of market ideology coupled with a paralyzing fear of further inflation seems to be blinding policy-makers to the opportunities for simultaneously serving different objectives of policy. Not *all* demand stimulants aggravate inflation on net balance.

That brings us to the second major charge against the proposed tax relief, namely, that much or even most of it will run off into added inflation. No one can deny that added dollars in consumers' hands will elicit some price increases. But in 1974, a year in which deficient demand will persist even after recovery replaces recession, the trade-off will be highly favorable. Consider the nature of today's inflation:

- Above all, it reflects price pressures born of the food and fuel shortages of yesteryear which do not, as Arthur Burns cogently pointed out in 1973, represent either the basic trend in prices or the response of prices to previous monetary-fiscal policies. Later this year, those pressures will begin to burn themselves out, leaving a legacy of high but less rapidly rising prices.
- In part, it is a lagged response to the boom in world commodity prices in general. And these pressures too will ebb even as demand recovers, much as they did after the price explosion set off by the Korean boom in 1951.
- Further, it is in some part the result of a sharp rise in unit labor costs, which moved ahead at a 9 percent annual rate in the last quarter of 1973 and will get worse in recession before getting better in recovery.

- Upward price adjustments as industries are freed from controls will also give inflation a jolt, largely a one-shot phenomenon.

In other words, inflation in 1974 has a life of its own, nourished not by excess demand but mainly by a variety of cost factors beyond the reach of fiscal and monetary management. The great bulk of the stimulus of a prompt tax cut would therefore express itself in higher output, jobs, and income, not in higher prices.

It can be argued—indeed, George Perry of Brookings has argued—that a well-tempered tax cut can help relieve cost-push pressure by redressing labor's cost-of-living grievances in part through tax relief rather than wage escalation. Labor leaders keep an eye closely cocked on that critical barometer, "real spendable earnings *after* taxes." Cut income and payroll taxes, and real earnings rise. If a fiscal bargain could be struck with labor to substitute this paycheck sweetener in part for wage hikes, less of the 1973–74 food and fuel price upsurge will be built into wage bargains.

But what about the legacy of a weakened tax system in 1975 and later years? Won't the inflationary chickens come home to roost? Not if responsive fiscal and monetary policies head off renewed excess demand when it again threatens the economy.

For that matter, the Congress should build in a large part of the protection by coupling its exemption boost with a firm commitment to enact compensating revenue-raising tax reforms to become effective in and beyond 1975. The necessary funds could be raised simply by a substantial hike in the minimum tax plus a phasing out of most of the tax shelters for petroleum as oil price curbs are progressively relaxed.

But one still has to confront the third question: Isn't Mr. Nixon's new budget already offering plenty of stimulus to a sagging economy? And besides, shouldn't we be reassured by OMB Director Ray Ash's promise to "bust the budget" if Mr. Nixon's exercise in exorcism fails and the economy is by recession repossessed? The answer is "no" on both counts.

True, the fiscal 1975 budget gives the *appearance* of stimulus. Spending is scheduled to rise $30 billion, and the deficit to double from $4.7 billion to $9.4 billion. But as this most realistic of Mr. Nixon's budget messages makes clear, "The recommended budget totals continue [the] policy of fiscal restraint as part of a continuing anti-inflation program." Indeed, the unified budget surplus on a full-employment basis would rise from $4 billion to $8 billion.

On a national income accounts basis, the rise in the full employment surplus would be even greater. Even without fully accepting the St. Louis Federal Reserve Bank numbers showing a rise in the full employment surplus from a rate of $2 billion in the first half of 1974 to nearly $13 billion in the first half of 1975, and even allowing for the inevitable slippage in the budget process, one can safely conclude that the fiscal 1975 budget, contrary to surface appearances, offers no substantial stimulus to the economy.

But what of the assurances that contingency plans will be rolled out to step up spending in case recession rears its ugly head? Given the typical lags in policy action and economic reaction, one can only say that the time to act is now. When a man is drowning, one should not deny him a life preserver on grounds that one can always resort to mouth-to-mouth resuscitation.

In the spring of 1974, Phase 4 wage-price controls were progressively fading from the scene, with the final curtain scheduled for April 30. The White House attitude was one of "good riddance," with only John Dunlop, Director of the Cost of Living Council, fighting a rear-guard action to salvage some selective statutory restraints during the post-Phase 4 period.

Deeply preoccupied with Watergate—how deeply only became known later—the White House lost most of its capacity for economic policy leadership. The theater of economic action shifted to the other end of Pennsylvania Avenue.

But Congress, by its nature not a very suitable instrument of leadership, was particularly hesitant to pick up the baton Mr. Nixon had dropped. Faced with a public disenchanted by the succession of phases and freezes, by a business community that was clearly fed up, and by a labor movement dead set against any vestige of restraint in the form of guidelines and jawboning, the Congress seemed ready to abandon ship. Even the bare minimum of providing for an orderly transition, reenacting stand-by authority, and setting up a watchdog agency was in jeopardy.

The Untimely Flight from Controls

THE WALL STREET JOURNAL *April 15, 1974*

Congress is about to outdo the White House in running away from the inflation problem:

- While correctly observing that business and labor are bitterly opposed to wage-price controls—and that consumer views range from skeptical to cynical—Congress is mistakenly sending such controls to the gas chamber rather than putting them in cold storage.
- While correctly concluding that broad-scale mandatory controls had outlived their usefulness in an excess-demand, shortage-plagued economy, Congress is mistakenly walking away from its responsibility to assert the public interest in price-wage moderation in an economy plagued by softening demand and rising unemployment.
- While correctly observing that the White House has done its level worst to discredit controls, Congress is mistakenly refusing even to give John Dunlop and the Cost of Living Council the leverage they need to insure that the pledges of price moderation and supply in-

creases made in exchange for early de-control by many industries will be redeemed.

Granting that controls are in ill repute, one wonders how Congress can explain to itself today—let alone to voters next fall—the discarding of all wage-price restraints in the face of record rates of inflation of 12 percent in the cost of living and 15 percent in wholesale prices (including an ominous 35 percent rate of inflation last month in industrial commodity prices). Is it the product of a growing "what's-the-use" attitude? Is it an implicit surrender to an inflation that is deemed in part to be woven into the institutional fabric of our economy and in part visited upon us by uncontrollable external forces like world food and material shortages and oil cartels? In short, is inflation now thought to be not just out of control but beyond our control?

An affirmative answer to these brooding questions seems to underlie Milton Friedman's recent economic streak—one which evokes surprise, astonishment, and disbelief in the best streaking tradition—from Smithian laissez-faire to Brazilian indexation. At present, we use the cost-of-living escalator selectively to protect 32 million Social Security and civil service beneficiaries and 13 million recipients of foodstamps and to hedge inflation bets in wage contracts for 10 percent of the labor force. Mr. Friedman would put all groups—those who profit from inflation and those who suffer from it alike—on the inflation escalator and thus help institutionalize our present double-digit rates of inflation.

Meanwhile, interest rates are soaring as Arthur Burns and the Fed man their lonely ramparts in the battle against inflation. With wage-price control headed for oblivion in the face of seething inflation, the Fed apparently views itself as the last bastion of inflation defense. So it is adding to the witches' brew by implicitly calling on unemployment and economic slack to help check the inflation spiral.

In this atmosphere, and deafened by the drumfire of powerful labor and business lobbies, Congress seems to have closed its mind to the legitimate continuing role of price-wage constraints. What is that role in an economy relying primarily, as it should, on the dictates of the marketplace?

First are the important transitional functions of the Cost of Living Council for which Mr. Dunlop, with vacillating support from the White House, asked congressional authority. In its new form after April 30 the Council would have:

- enforced commitments made by the cement, fertilizer, auto, tire and tube, and many other de-controlled industries to restrain prices and-or expand supplies—commitments that would become unenforceable when COLC goes down the drain with the Economic Stabilization Act on April 30;
- protected patients against an explosion of hospital fees by keeping mandatory controls on the health-care industry until Congress adopts a national health insurance plan;
- prevented an early explosion of construction wages and the associated danger that housing recovery might be crippled;
- maintained veto power over wage bargains that are eligible for reopening when mandatory controls are lifted.

Beyond Phase 4's post-operative period, government needs to assert its presence in wage-price developments in several critical ways.

The first would be to continue the important function of monitoring other government agencies, of keeping a wary anti-inflationary eye on their farm, labor, trade, transport, energy and housing policies. The point is to protect consumers from the price consequences of the cost-boosting and price-propping activities of the producer-oriented agencies. The White House could continue this function without congressional authority, but a statutory base would give the watchdog agency much more clout.

Second would be the task of working with industry, labor, and government units to improve wage bargaining and relieve bottleneck inflation by encouraging increased production of scarce goods and raw materials.

Third, and by far the most important, would be the monitoring of major wage bargains and price decisions and spotlighting those that flout the public interest.

The trauma of Phases 3 and 4 has apparently blotted out memories of the painfully relevant experience of 1969–71:

- The school's-out, hands-off policy announced by Mr. Nixon early in 1969 touched off a rash of price increases and let a vicious wage-price spiral propel inflation upward even while the economy was moving downward.
- Only when Mr. Nixon finally moved in with the powerful circuit-breaker of the 90-day freeze was the spiral turned off.

Today, the urgent task is to see that it's not turned on again. In that quest, some forces are working in our favor:

- Much of the steam should be going out of special-sector inflation in oil, food, and raw materials.
- The pop-up or bubble effect of ending mandatory controls should work its inflationary way through the economy by the end of the year.
- As yet, wage settlements show few signs of shooting upwards as they did in 1969–70, when first-year increases jumped from 8 percent to 16 percent in less than a year. Wage moderation in 1973—induced in part by wage controls, but even more by the absence of inordinate profits in most labor-intensive industries and by the fact that the critical bottlenecks were in materials and manufacturing capacity rather than in labor supply—has set no high pay targets for labor to shoot at.

- Thus far in 1974, the aluminum, can, and newly signed steel settlements won't greatly boost those targets. So the wage-wage spiral is not yet at work. Since, in addition, cost-of-living escalators apply to only one-tenth of the U.S. work force, the ballooning cost of living has not yet triggered a new price-wage spiral. Still there is a distinct calm-before-the-storm feeling abroad in the land of labor negotiations.

With demand softening and shortages easing in large segments of the economy, the old rules of the marketplace would suggest that inflation is bound to moderate. And the odds are that it will—but how fast, how far, and how firmly is another matter. And that's where a price-wage monitor with a firm statutory base is badly needed. It could play a significant role in inducing big business to break the heady habit of escalating prices and in forestalling big labor's addiction to double-digit wage advances.

Industry after industry has gotten into the habit of raising prices on a cost-justified basis as energy, food, and raw material prices skyrocketed. Decontrol will reinforce that habit.

Once these bulges have worked their way through the economy, we tend to assume that virulent inflation will subside. Indeed, in some areas such as retailing, farm products, small business, and much of unorganized labor, competitive market forces will operate to help business and labor kick the inflationary habit.

But in areas dominated by powerful unions and industrial oligopolies, a prod is needed if habitual inflation— inflation with no visible means of support from underlying supply and demand conditions in the economy—is to be broken. If it is not, the threat of a wage break-out will loom large in upcoming wage negotiations in the construction, communications, aerospace, ship building, airlines, mining, and railroad industries. In those critical negotiations, the wage moderation of the past two years could go up in smoke if the ebbing of non-labor cost pressures is simply converted into profits rather than being shared with consumers in price moderation.

Congress and the White House are taking undue risks if they rely entirely on market forces to achieve this end, especially in those large areas of the economy where competitive forces are not strong enough to protect the consumer. To serve as his ombudsman and to help prevent the picking of his pocket by a management-labor coalition, the consumer needs a watch-dog agency that will bark and growl and occasionally bite. Such an agency—which could accomplish a good deal by skillful exercise of the powers of inquiry and publicity and much more if it were able to draw, sparingly, on powers of suspension and rollback when faced with gross violations and defiance—could provide substantial insurance against inflation by habit.

An action program to accomplish the foregoing would have included—indeed, given a miracle of courage, conviction and speed, could still include—the following elements:

- A quick and simple extension of the standby powers of the Economic Stabilization Act.
- Granting of the authority requested by John Dunlop for the transitional period.
- The establishment of a monitoring agency—preferably by statute and equipped with last-resort suspension and rollback powers, but if that is not to be, then by White House action and relying mainly on instruments of inquiry and publicity—to look over the shoulder of big business and big labor on behalf of the consumer.

To declare open season on wage-price decisions under present circumstances—as we seem hell-bent to do in our disenchantment with controls and sudden revival of faith in the market system—would be one more example of the classic action-reaction pattern that excludes the middle way. The Congress and the country may well rue the day when, largely at the behest of big business and organized labor, the government presence in their price and wage decisions was mindlessly liquidated, leaving the consumer to fend for himself.

As the floodtide of U.S. and worldwide inflation moved toward its high-water mark in the summer of 1974, even while recession deepened, the search for remedies or devices to cope with the situation intensified. Sparked by Milton Friedman (after a visit to Brazil), a boomlet developed for "indexation." In Brazil, one of the most inflation-prone economies of the world, indexing seemed to have played a significant role in pulling inflation down while economic growth accelerated. Was it all that it seemed? And would it thrive as a transplant to the United States?

Has the Time Come for Indexing?

THE WALL STREET JOURNAL *June 20, 1974*

In a world caught in the toils of unrelenting inflation, it is small wonder that "indexing" or "indexation" is gaining attention and adherents.

The idea of using a general price index to translate fluctuating money values of payments like wages and interest and of assets like bonds and savings into stable real values is not new, of course. A century ago, the English economist Jevons was searching for just such a stable standard of values. And in recent years, Belgium, Israel and Finland have indexed wages, pensions, rents, and a wide range of financial transactions.

Even in the United States, we practice indexing in a limited way. Cost-of-living adjustments provide some insurance against inflation for 32 million Social Security and civil service beneficiaries and 13 million recipients of food stamps. And the wages of about 10 percent of the labor force are at least partly hedged against inflation by cost-of-living escalators.

What is new is not indexing as such, but the proposal

that it be applied across the board. Struck by Brazil's heady economic experience, Milton Friedman urges us to "express all transactions that have a time duration in terms that eliminate the effect of inflation." This, it is claimed, would automatically take both the sting and the honey out of inflation and clear the path for monetary and fiscal measures to bring it under control.

Brazil's widespread use of indexing, or what it calls "monetary correction," has coincided with a marked slow-down in inflation and a strong speed-up in growth. The annual rate of inflation was brought down from about 90 percent in 1964 to 15 percent in 1973 (though world-wide inflationary pressures have again pushed it up to over 35 percent in the early months of 1974). Meanwhile, real growth has averaged better than 10 percent a year since 1968.

But has indexing really been the hero of the piece? Does the Brazilian experience apply to conditions in the U.S. ? For much of the following analysis I am indebted to Professor Albert Fishlow at the University of California.

After the military takeover in 1964, Brazil applied indexing with a vengeance in an effort to cope with rampant inflation and to get financial markets back on their feet:

- Indexes measuring inflation rates of the recent past are used to translate money values into real values for payments of rent, interest and taxes as well as for assets like bonds, savings accounts and both the fixed and working capital of business.
- Wage increases are determined by applying an index of expected future price and productivity increases to a base consisting of the average real wages paid in the preceding 24 months.
- Profits are determined on the basis of real gains after monetary correction, while the level of exemptions and the range of tax brackets under the personal income tax are redefined each year in accordance with price level changes.

- The foreign exchange rate was put on a crawling peg, a system of regular mini-devaluations geared to the differential rate of Brazilian inflation.

The measure of inflation generally used for the correction process is the wholesale commodity price index (except in the case of rentals, where the minimum wage is used as the indexing standard). Apart from wages, where the index is applied in an arbitrary way, the system is far from automatic. To implement changes in economic policy, the authorities have adjusted tax privileges, loan repayment terms and real interest rate levels from time to time.

Wage indexing, as used in Brazil, was not a device to help labor keep pace with inflation. In fact, the wage formula, especially during the early years, had a built-in bias toward a reduction of real wages, partly because the correction for future inflation (and productivity advances) substantially undershot the mark and partly because rampant inflation eroded the calculated wage base. As a result, real minimum wages declined some 16 percent in the first phase of the program up to 1967. In the following five years, average wage gains covered only half to two-thirds of productivity advances. Only in 1972 and 1973 did rough parity prevail.

No one disputes that the Brazilian economy has made impressive strides in the decade since indexation was introduced. But the closer one looks, the clearer it becomes that indexing—in the usually accepted sense of impartial and automatic adjustments to general price movements— made only a marginal contribution to that success. Several facts lead inescapably to this conclusion.

First, the decisive role in reducing Brazil's inflation was played not by indexing but by (a) fiscal discipline that reduced the cash deficit from more than 4 percent of total output in 1963 to a small surplus in 1973; (b) price and wage controls; (c) the large productivity dividends produced by high rates of growth, and (d) greater international openness and the resulting competitive pressures on the domestic economy.

Second, Brazil's in-name-only indexation for wages was actually a formula for unwinding inflation at the expense of labor. The substantial decline in real wages, especially in the lower income groups, bears witness to this.

Third, from the foregoing it is clear that the important parts of the program bearing the label "monetary correction" did not serve the cause of equity under conditions of rapid price rise—which presumably is the name of the game in indexing—but precisely the opposite.

Fourth, far from being an automatic correction based on overall price movements and thereby serving as a neutral "rule" to supplant governmental authority in allocating resources and distributing income, Brazilian indexing has been highly discretionary. To think otherwise does not do credit to the ingenuity and innovativeness of Brazilian policymakers. It fails to convey the degree to which rapid growth and disinflation were a product of conscious intervention in the economy.

Fifth, as recognized by such respected Brazilian authorities as Minister of Finance Mario Enrique Simonson, indexing eliminates the usual frictions in the inflationary process and thus may become a "feedback factor" in the rate of price increases. The 1974 jump in Brazil's inflation rate stemming from the global rise in food and energy prices seems to illustrate this point. The country's nimble policymakers already are investigating new ways of blocking this transmission effect.

Although indexing played a minor direct role in Brazil's successes on the growth and inflation fronts, it did help set the stage. By restoring and guaranteeing positive real rates of interest to savers, it helped revive capital markets and created the conditions in which new financial institutions could work, thus enabling the market to allocate resources more efficiently. Also, with the help of a broad range of export subsidies and incentives, the crawling-peg exchange rate facilitated a truly impressive growth in Brazil's exports. These consequences were important for Brazil's economic advance. But they are largely irrelevant to a U.S. economy blessed with strong financial institutions and foreign trade.

Indeed, the adjustment of interest rates to inflation via the marketplace, as in the U.S., affords an interesting contrast with adjustments by indexing. What is the greater wisdom? To escalate long-term interest rates via indexing in response to the 1973–74 food and fuel price explosion? Or temporarily to offer a negative return on long-term money as our sophisticated capital markets are doing? These markets seem to be telling us that we should not build today's inflation into tomorrow's expectations on an exactly proportionate basis (nor, for that matter, should we ignore projected earnings in the productive sector).

An automatic across-the-board indexing system would have promptly translated skyrocketing commodity prices not only into higher interest rates but into higher wages. Thus, it would have put relentless cost-push pressure on the general price level. Under the present system, one has at least a fighting chance to avoid converting the 1973–74 "soft core" inflation—food, fuel, industrial materials and post-Phase 4 pop-up inflation—into a "hard core" price-wage spiral reaching well into the future.

Because of its uneven impacts, then, our existing system throws sand into the gears of inflation. Indexing would oil the gears and speed the process of inflation.

Under the present circumstances, a good case can be made for using cost-of-living escalators in wage bargains instead of building the present rate of inflation into those contracts. Labor is thus protected against high rates of inflation, while the public is assured that wages won't be pegged at levels that ignore declining rates of inflation.

But it should be recognized that if across-the-board indexing of wages were required, vexing questions would arise. Would the base, or take-off point, simply be the existing wage level, or would adjustments have to be made for previous wage erosion and wage inequities? Would some nationwide adjustment for productivity also have to be prescribed? And would that not call for price-monitoring?

Beyond this, could a cost-of-living index be tuned finely enough to maintain the even-handedness that is a major objective of indexing? It is probably beyond the capacity of an indexing system, for example, to adjust for the fact that inroads of zooming food and fuel prices have been more serious for modest and low incomes than for high incomes.

Or consider the difficulties in trying to index income tax liabilities as Brazil has done:

- Suppose we adjusted personal exemptions and the width of the tax brackets by the cost-of-living index today. It would give too much relief to those for whom food and fuel absorb only a small percentage of income and vice versa.
- A tax fix via indexing cuts tax liabilities for those hurt by inflation but imposes no penalties on those, like debtors, who are helped by it.
- Indexing reduces the automatic stabilizing force that a progressive income tax exerts by taking more money out of an inflationary economy. In this sense it demands more of discretionary fiscal policy.

Indexing would also throw a heavier burden on conventional fiscal, monetary and wage-price policies because it is such an efficient "conductor" of the inflationary impact of outside shocks like the quadrupling of Arab oil prices. Such policies are having a hard enough time trying to curb existing inflation without making them compensate for indexation as well.

This is not to say that indexation has no role to play in the U.S. economy. As the Social Security and food stamp examples illustrate, it has definite attractions as a means of buffering the incomes of groups who have no built-in protection against inflation. Cost-of-living escalators for wages can also play a useful role in an economy where inflationary forces are ebbing. And the federal government might want to issue an indexed security itself and remove legal barriers to private indexing arrangements in financial transactions. Having "purchasing power bonds" as an option would enable the system to respond more efficiently to differential expectations of future inflation among investors and thereby reduce nominal interest rates.

But even with the best of intentions and the most perfect of applications, indexing cannot fairly lay claim to being neutral, automatic or highly equitable. It does not do away with either market power or political power. But it does do away with some of the inhibitions against inflation and some of the frictions that serve as circuit-breakers to slow it down.

In short, carefully targeted indexing in small doses can promote equity without worsening inflation. But in large doses, it is more likely to be an opiate than a cure for inflation.

By the summer of 1974, it seemed that not only Watergate but the economy too was unraveling. Inflation was rampant. Instead of turning up, the economy continued its slide into recession. And economic policy was in a state of near-paralysis.

Consumer prices raced ahead at a record 15 percent annual pace by mid-summer. (See Chart 4.) Especially after the blanket of wage-price controls was thrown off, the inflationary fever spread to commodities other than food and fuel and to medical, household, and other services.

The blinding glare of inflation served to mask the economic recession that was stealthily gnawing at the economy's vitals. Or at least, the fear of being branded soft on inflation served to stay the hand of Congress, while the White House was immobilized by the trials and tribulations of Watergate.

But it was more than that. Such indicators as unemployment rates and factory order books strangely failed to reflect the deterioration of the economy. Real GNP (in stable dollars) was easing off throughout 1974—as

Chart 4. Prices, 1968–1976
Seasonally Adjusted

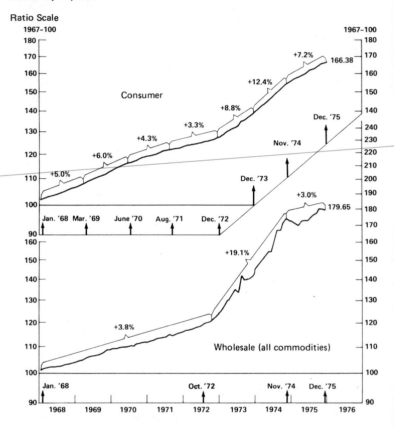

Source: U.S. Department of Labor and Federal Reserve Bank of St. Louis

were industrial production, real income and investment—and the housing industry was hard hit by high interest rates and tight money. Yet the unemployment rate, after a jump from its low point of 4.6 percent in October 1973 to 5.2 percent in January 1974, held almost steady for six months. Apparently misled by bulging (indeed, inflated) order books and repeated Administration assurances that the economic slowdown would soon be over, employers were loath to lay off workers.

It was not until fall that the bubble burst. As the recession gained momentum and orders backlogs collapsed in a rash of cancellations, the deluge of dismissals began and unemployment jumped. (See Chart 5.)

Don't such events cast their shadows before? Some economists thought so and responded accordingly to the anxious inquiries of Congressional committees. Testifying before the Joint Economic Committee on August 1, I noted that the Nixon Administration, "in speaking glibly of a 'phantom recession,' is missing the point. . . . Undeviating adherence to present policies will push unemployment closer to 7 percent next winter than the 6 percent that is currently being forecast."

Just eight days later, Gerald R. Ford, the country's first appointed President, took over from the disgraced

Chart 5. Unemployment rates, 1968–1976 (seasonally adjusted)

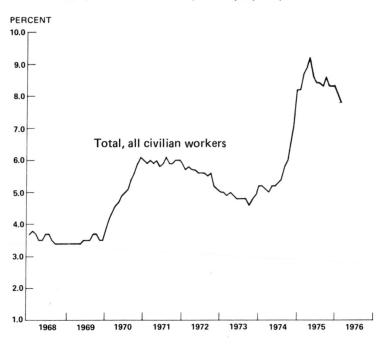

PERCENT

Total, all civilian workers

Source: U.S. Department of Labor and Federal Reserve Bank of St. Louis

Richard Nixon. An end to policy paralysis was now in sight. And President Ford entered office with an unprecedentedly clean slate. The temptation to suggest what economic policies he might write on that slate was more than this member of *The Wall Street Journal* Board of Contributors could resist.

An Open Letter to President Ford

THE WALL STREET JOURNAL *August 12, 1974*

As you enter the presidency, the Number 1 problem on your domestic docket is inflation. In tackling it you have an opportunity that has come only once in the lifetime of this republic, one that enables you to make a New Beginning, backed by the will, the support, and the hopes of the vast majority of Americans.

It's an odds-on bet that the present corps of economic advisers will recommend that you use this priceless opportunity to maintain unflinching adherence to the "old-time religion," to the catharsis of tight money and budget cutting.

But before you accept that counsel and the appealing Rock of Gibraltar image it implies, you should take a fresh hard look at the inflation problem, bearing in mind the new options that open up as you restore credibility and integrity to the White House. No one expects you to find a quick, magic cure for inflation—there are none. But people rightfully expect you to ask the tough, searching questions that will reveal the true risks and rewards of present policies and point the way to a broader and better balanced anti-inflation program.

A nagging question pops up at the outset: Why should the economic game plan that failed so miserably in 1968–71 work in 1974–75? Tightening the fiscal and then monetary screws generated 6 percent unemployment and the recession of 1970, yet failed to subdue inflation. But, you will be told, that's because "we failed to stay the long course."

At that point, it's fair to ask how deep a valley of disinflation lies ahead of us under present policy. What the President, the Congress, and the public need is a candid calculation—free of self-delusions and false optimism—of the projected benefits and costs of monetary-fiscal austerity:

- How much inflation will it squeeze out of the economy, and by when?
- How much will it cost in lost jobs, output, and profits and in business and financial failures?

Careful econometric studies by James Tobin and by Otto Eckstein of Data Resources provide a partial and chilling answer. They agree that the cost of simply adhering to severe monetary and fiscal restraint to check inflation will be sustained and heavy unemployment. Mr. Eckstein calculates that it would take *at least* two years of 8 percent unemployment to beat inflation back to a 4 percent rate. I think you will agree with him, Mr. President, this would be "overkill" and that "the financial system would collapse before we cracked inflation."

That raises a closely allied question: Given the kind of inflation we are suffering today, are demand-suppressing measures enough? Are they the right medicine for this inflation? I don't mean to say that understanding how the inflation genie got out of the bottle necessarily tells us how to get it back in. But surely the medicine—and the dosage—should be different if inflation is merely a lingering legacy of demand-pull forces than if specific supply crunches and cost-push forces are the villains.

The plain fact is that 1974 inflation, born of 1973's combination of excessive demand and commodity crunches, is rapidly maturing into a new spiral of wages chasing prices and prices chasing wages—into a self-propelling price-wage spiral all too reminiscent of 1969–70 and all too resistant to a monetary-fiscal squeeze. The result? Further turns of the monetary and fiscal screws will wring less and less inflation and more and more life blood out of our economic recovery.

This is becoming painfully evident as the first-half slide turns into second-half torpor. Every day new cracks are appearing in the façade of economic strength behind which the ordained optimists have been hiding. A first step toward more realistic policy must be to recognize the 1974 slump for what it is: Not merely an "energy spasm," "a shortages economy," or a pause that refreshes, but a costly stagnation arising out of a shortfall in aggregate demand.

Let's drop the debate over whether it deserves the label "recession" and redirect our attention to the real problems: How far below our output and employment potential are we prepared to drive the economy by policies to cut demand?

For the longer pull, much of the relief from stubborn inflation must come from the supply side. An intensive review of government policy to enlarge critical supply capacities, increase productivity, and monitor emerging supply crunches is long overdue.

In light of our traumatic experience with shortages in the last couple of years, you should call for a thorough exploration of the potentials for supply management. This should range all the way from better information devices like shortage alerts and prompt export reports or even licensing to the use of special financial aids (without building new tax shelters) and the milder forms of credit rationing.

Rationing of credit by price alone is channeling too much of our limited financial resources into speculative investment in land, inventories, and foreign exchange to the detriment of investment in productive capital. And, as always, super-tight credit is squeezing small business, housing, and municipal borrowers. To curb such inequities and channel more credit into productive uses, Federal Reserve policy should, where feasible, apply more selective methods of supplying credit.

And a gradual phaseout of the Regulation Q ceilings (the

Federal Reserve Board's limits on interest rates payable on various classes of savings accounts) that shortchange small savers and distort the flow of financial resources is clearly in order. These moves would facilitate the gradual retreat from excessive tightness that is needed to permit a moderate economic expansion.

A government that is dead serious about fighting inflation ought also, at long last, under your leadership, to put an end to the laws, regulations, and practices that make government an accomplice in many cost- and price-propping actions. They run from over-regulation of transportation rates and under-enforcement of antitrust laws to fair trade laws and the Davis-Bacon Act (requiring, in effect, that union wages—i.e., the highest wages prevailing in each area—be paid on any construction project financed in whole or in part with federal funds)—not to mention maritime subsidies, import quotas, and the Buy American Act. Such actions will step on the toes of articulate, well-heeled pressure groups—but now is the time to take those political risks.

And in view of the limits of demand management policy in subduing the new inflation, what measures to curb cost-push pressures and to improve supply management should now be considered?

Here, above all, Mr. President, you are in a unique position to de-escalate the inflationary spiral. Labor, justifiably aggrieved about the erosion of its real earnings, is stepping up its demands. Business, also pointing to inflation inroads and citing huge capital needs, is pushing up prices and profit margins. Now is the time, backed by a floodtide of goodwill, to practice not just the politics but the economics of reconciliation. Now is the time to bring business and labor together in a dialogue, leading under your guidance to economic détente for the benefit of the American consumer.

That will mean reaching out to bring labor back into the fold. It will require evidence that the strong pro-business bias of recent White House economics will become not a pro-labor but a pro-public bias. And it will also require a liberal (or even conservative) dash of the "reasoning together" and "ask not . . ." spirit that seems to underlie your early words and actions as President.

Translating this new mood into specific initiatives to defuse the price-wage spiral won't be easy, especially after the unfortunate discrediting of wage-price controls under the inept freezes and phases of recent history. But without some kind of a wage-price watchdog and a new set of evenhanded wage-price guides—backed not just by powers of inquiry and publicity but by powers of suspension (and in outrageous cases even by rollbacks)—the outlook for inserting a circuit-breaker in the new round of cost-push inflation will remain bleak. Building on the base of the Bentsen-Nixon proposals for a wage-price monitoring agency, the White House and Congress can forge this missing link in the anti-inflation chain.

This may go against your free-market instincts, Mr. President. But it shouldn't. Monitoring would be focused on those powerful unions and business units that wield excessive market power, those areas of the economy where competition is a poor policeman; in other words, the government presence would be a stand-in for the forces of competition.

While dealing with the supply side of the equation, let me emphasize how important it is not to undermine some of our natural defenses against inflation by stopping expansion dead in its tracks. For if we do, we would deny ourselves the short-run peoductivity offsets to rising costs that we normally reap from a rising volume of sales and output. The longer we stunt productivity by choking off recovery, the more likely it is that lower productivity growth and hence higher unit costs will be built into conventional markups.

Further, remember that investment, innovation, and risk-taking thrive in an atmosphere of expansion and wither in an atmosphere of stagnation. Super-tight credit undermines the health of equity markets, pushes money costs skyward, and threatens profits and financial stability. In the face of a policy of calculated stagnation, no program of tax gimmicks or special incentives will be able to induce the increases in capital spending the nation needs to boost productivity, expand supplies, and ease price pressures.

Finally, Mr. President, in formulating your anti-inflationary program, be sure to take it out of the narrow context of economic gains and losses into the broader perspective of its social impact, of the inequities and unfairness that it could generate. Out of these inequities grow a sense of grievance and alienation, an undermining of morale and social cohesion that may be inflation's greatest cost.

A telling reason why so many segments of our society have rejected current policies—have indeed felt they add up to an anti-them instead of an anti-inflation program—is that they are its victims rather than its beneficiaries.

Monetary policy boosts their housing costs. Budget policy has been squeezing social programs while enlarging defense outlays. And tax policy has thus far shown too little concern for those who are being shortchanged by inflation.

A truly balanced attack on inflation would couple the restraints of fiscal and monetary policy with measures to redress the grievances of skyrocketing fuel and food prices. I urge you to consider as an integral part of a compassionate anti-inflation program not only more generous unemployment benefits, food stamps, and housing allowances but relief from payroll taxes for the working poor and increases in personal income tax exemptions and low income allowances. Distributing the benefits and burdens of economic policy more fairly will facilitate a more sustained battle against inflation.

If we simply declare total war against inflation without weighing the resulting devastation of the human and financial landscape, experience tells us that we will invite an eventual public backlash. This is a plea, not to be soft on inflation, but to strike a sensible balance between benefits and costs in your anti-inflationary program, thereby staying within the bounds of economic and political tolerance rather than risking repudiation of the battle before it is won.

Just one final thought: I realize that if you follow the foregoing counsel, it will enhance the prospects of your continuation in the presidency after 1976. But in the belief that partisanship stops at inflation's edge, that's a risk I'll have to take.*

On September 5, at the first of the "mini-summit conferences" that were part of the unprecedented White House Conference on Inflation, President Ford ringingly repeated to the twenty-eight economists who were gathered at the White House—and to the nation, listening on TV—his inaugural theme that "Inflation is Public Enemy Number One." Many of the conferees in the intensive series of meetings that September were in agreement. But others urged that unemployment and recession be given equal or perhaps even higher priority.**

The following statement at the final "summit conference" is an attempt to draw together a few of the significant threads and themes of the mini-summit conferences and weave them into a policy pattern appropriate to an economy plagued by stagflation.

Remarks on Inflation

WHITE HOUSE "SUMMIT CONFERENCE" *September 28, 1974*

Contrary to the skeptics—and in spite of my view that the economists' second mini-summit "lived down to my expectations"—I think this month of summitry has already

---

* During an informal conversation in early September at the first of a series of White House conferences on inflation, the President was gracious enough to say that he had read the "open letter" with interest. But if one is to judge by his later policy recommendations, he did not find it very persuasive!
** See Part II, pages 173–74, for comments on some of the areas of agreement among the economists at the White House conferences.

made its mark. Let me cite chapter and verse on this conclusion and some suggestions for making the summit effort even more productive.

1. It has led to a new candor in facing up to the grisly facts
   not just of stubborn inflation but of a menacing recession. Granted, it is upsetting to the public and even to
   the stock market to face at long last the dismal facts of
   economic life. But that's an essential first step to a solution.
2. The mini-summit meetings have made crystal-clear that
   the Federal Reserve, in trying to wring the inflationary
   water out of the economy, has been squeezing too
   much of the productive lifeblood out of it. The Fed has
   backed off a bit. But without throwing restraint to the
   winds, it should back off still more.

   One mini-summit after another emphasized that the
   present degree of monetary tightness is both painful
   and dangerous. It is strangling the housing industry,
   threatening financial institutions, pinching small business, starving public utilities, devastating the stock
   market, squeezing foreign economies, endangering capital expansion, undermining consumer credit, and
   choking off economic recovery. If that's not tight
   money, "it don't snow in Minneapolis in the winter-
   time."
3. The summit has borne in on both the White House and
   the Congress the vital need to broaden the scope of the
   inflation program, to recognize that the inequities of
   inflation are even more damaging than its economic
   inefficiency. Tax and budget relief for those (especially
   the poor and the elderly) who have been victimized by
   exploding food and fuel prices and for the casualties of
   fiscal-monetary austerity (like the jobless and the housing industry) not only got on the agenda during the
   summit process, but are apparently rising steadily toward the top. President Ford's and Alan Greenspan's
   support of tax relief to the poor confirms this.

But such tax relief must be made meaningful and *not offset* with new consumption taxes on the poor. Let the closing of tax escapes, especially for the oil industry, together with prudent budget pruning, provide the necessary funds.

4. Also, it has been brought home that simply suppressing consumer, business, and government demand can't do the anti-inflationary job without unbearable costs and inequity. More specifically, impressive arithmetic and econometrics have been brought forward to show that budget cuts of $5 to $10 billion don't offer much payoff in reduced inflation.

To the extent that these conclusions are widely accepted by objective observers (by my definition of "objective," of course), it follows that a policy of monetary-fiscal restraint must be flanked by a broad spectrum of other measures:

- New measures must be taken to improve supply management, avert shortages, and translate "boosts in productivity" from rhetoric to reality.
- More selective measures must be taken, for example, in the allocation of credit. The new guidelines issued by the Federal Reserve's advisory committee represent the first tentative step to distinguish between productive and speculative uses of funds. The Federal Reserve should follow this up by making more explicit rules to guide funds into productive investment, housing, and small business and away from speculative investment in inventories, foreign exchange, land, and corporate takeovers.
- More effective price-wage restraint must accompany the moderating of monetary-fiscal restraint.
- Some of those "sacred cows" by which government props up prices and costs must now be slain.

5. A list of 22 of these sacred cows that should be slaughtered has been overwhelmingly endorsed by the group

with the least axes to grind—the professional economists, predominantly from academic life. The group
called for ending restrictions like import quotas, "fair
trade" laws, over-regulation of railroads and airlines,
and a whole list of other restrictions, subsidies, and pro-
tections which make government an accomplice in
mugging the consumer.

A painful and current case in point is the bill just
passed by Congress to require 30 percent of U.S. oil imports to be carried in U.S. flag tankers, which will cost
American consumers hundreds of millions of dollars.
One hopes that this fatted calf will be stillborn. [Presi-
dent Ford did veto this bill.]

No President has had the temerity to take on the
special interest groups that are quietly picking the consumer's pocket with the government's help. But then,
no modern President has had to face unyielding double-
digit inflation in peacetime, and no President has entered the White House less beholden to special interests
than President Ford.

6. On the wage-price front, no clear consensus has
emerged from the summit process. Without an effective
effort to black the new price-wage spiral that is growing
out of the 1973–74 explosion in the cost of living, the
battle against inflation cannot be won for years to come.

It is vital to give the Council on Wage and Price Stability some teeth. This new price-wage watchdog can do
some good by barking and growling—especially if the
President himself says "sic-'em" from time to time. But
it would be far more effective if it could bite big business and powerful labor unions when they defy the
public interest. This requires powers of subpoena, powers of suspension, and in cases of flagrant rip-offs of the
public, powers of denial and rollback. If we fail to short-
circuit that price-wage spiral now, the demands of the
American people for a full-scale straitjacket of controls—which most of us want to avoid—will become
well-nigh irresistible.

7. Public service jobs, expanded unemployment compensation, and broadscale job training are now widely endorsed as landing nets for those knocked out of jobs by tight money and tight budgets. In designing these programs, I hope the designers will bear in mind the groups whose jobs or job opportunities shrivel up first under the blows of monetary-fiscal austerity. For example, compared with average unemployment:

- white teenagers are three times as likely to be unemployed;
- black teenagers, six times;
- blacks as a whole, twice;
- the poor, also twice.

When employment is full and labor markets are tight, the sheer self-interest of employers drives them at last to hire those at the bottom of the job barrel. When jobs are scarce and getting scarcer, as in 1974–75, the government's efforts on the public service jobs and training fronts have to focus on these groups, give them skills and experience in meaningful tasks, and thus enlarge the effective work force that will be available to meet job demands when prosperity returns.

8. Along with all the do's, there's one important don't. Don't fasten on the American consumer the additional inflationary ransom of $5–10 billion that would be involved in freeing the price of "old" domestic oil from its present $5.25 controlled level. To do so would give the oil companies, in the ringing words of Justice Frankfurter in another context, "a plain, unvarnished luscious bonanza of a windfall."

On an earlier occasion, I had drawn up an illustrative agenda of specific measures that would help reduce the conflict between high employment and price stability. Since that agenda remained nearly intact two years later—and since it supplies chapter and verse on some of the structural changes advocated at the Summit Con-

ference on Inflation—it seemed useful to append it to
the foregoing Summit statement.

A Program to Improve the Trade-off Between Unemployment and Inflation

HEARING BEFORE THE JOINT ECONOMIC
COMMITTEE U.S. CONGRESS *July 27, 1972*

A balanced program to shift the Phillips Curve—to better the trade-off between unemployment and inflation—
would include at least four types of measures:

1. *Semi-voluntary wage-price restraints* applicable to concentrated industries and powerful labor unions.
2. *Measures to step up the increase in productivity* (i.e.,
   getting more output per unit of input) by increased investment in human brainpower and skills, in plant and
   equipment, and in research and development. (This category overlaps somewhat with numbers 3 and 4.)
3. *Labor market policy:* Manpower training, development,
   and placement, including the whole array of pre-job,
   on-the-job, and between-jobs training and retraining;
   an improved and nationalized system of labor
   exchanges; specialized job-creation programs—public
   service jobs, youth opportunities, and the like—with
   emphasis on jobs for young people, nonwhites, women,
   and other groups with a high incidence of unemployment; and adaptation of jobs to people, i.e., redesigning
   jobs in at least two ways, (a) to make some jobs more
   available to less skilled and experienced workers and (b)
   to make other jobs more challenging and less routine as
   a means of motivating skilled and experienced workers.
4. *Structural changes to remove rigidities and impediments to efficient, least-cost ways of doing things and
   to pull out artificial props that operate to hold prices at
   unnaturally high levels.* The actions required here com-

prise a long, demanding, and politically painful list, for example,

- removing import quotas;
- renegotiating tariff rates;
- repealing the Davis-Bacon Act;
- eliminating featherbedding and other restrictive labor practices;
- modernizing and liberalizing archaic local building codes;
- eliminating racial discrimination in jobs and in educational, training, and placement facilities that lead to jobs (measures that have been estimated to add about 4 percent a year to GNP);
- intensifying antitrust activities;
- reducing farm price supports and redesigning farm subsidies to minimize their price-push effects;
- reforming our income tax laws to reduce or remove tax shelters for oil and gas, commercial housing, mining, hobby farming, and the like, i.e., cut back the "tax expenditure" subsidies that pull resources out of their natural channels into less efficient tax-favored pursuits;
- eliminate "fair trade" laws (which, according to recent estimates, add about three tenths of a percentage point to the consumer price index);
- in the field of transportation rates, rely more heavily on competition among and within various modes of transportation as a substitute for the relatively ineffectual regulatory processes that now obtain.

Reading the foregoing program several years later, one should take some small comfort in the disappearance, in whole or part, of several items from the agenda:

- The Congress in 1975, with President Ford's approval, wiped the fair trade law from the books—an action long sought by economists of all persuasions.

- After the dramatic rise in oil prices in 1973–74, percentage depletion allowances for oil, the kingpin of tax "loopholes," were eliminated for large oil companies in 1975.
- Responding to the shift from grain glut to grain shortage and the consequent skyrocketing of grain prices, the Administration and Congress had also, in 1973, veered sharply away from traditional price supports, phased out agricultural export subsidies, and curtailed import restrictions.

Perhaps the most wholesome, if undramatic, upshot of the summit conferences was the triggering of White House initiatives to cut back some of the government over-regulation that undermines competition and efficiency. Indeed, close advisers of President Ford reported that the 24 economists' "Manifesto" was the immediate spur to action.

The most important thrust of regulatory reform was aimed at the transportation industry.* As President Ford put it in his 1976 *Economic Report:* "My object is to achieve a better combination of market competition and responsible government regulation. . . . I have asked the Congress to legislate fundamental changes in the laws regulating our railroads, airlines, and trucking firms. The new amendments will free these companies to respond more flexibly to market conditions."

The President called for more 'freedom for carriers to raise and lower their rates without government approval, for greater freedom to enter transportation markets and to drop uneconomic services, and for a cutback in regulators' power to grant antitrust immunity to truckers. As brought out in Part II (pages 174–75), these moves have widespread support in the economics profession.

Even in the early weeks of the new Administration, it became clear that Mr. Ford and the economic team he had inherited—and retained—would take a hard line on

---

* For illuminating discussions of the rationale and progress of "the deregulation movement" in industry and agriculture, see Chapters 5 and 6 of *The Economic Report of the President,* February 1975.

budget spending and deficits. Time and again during the summit conferences, the Ford team pointed accusingly at the budget as the source of all (or most) inflationary evil. Time and again, the President and his cohorts called for cutting the fiscal 1975 budget from its then-programed level of nearly $310 billion back to "below $300 billion."

The implication was clear: recession or no, budget cutbacks were the path of economic virtue. The following article was an attempt to separate fiction from fact, myth from reality, in federal budgeting, a field where public misperception and faulty reasoning abound.

Budget Cutting and Inflation

As the month of economic summitry draws to a close and the White House draws from it some guidelines for presidential action, budget-chopping seems to be high on the agenda. But before Mr. Ford and the Congress conclude that the budget is the taproot of today's inflation and decide on budget-cutting as their chosen path out of the inflationary wilderness, they should take a hard look at the "facts" and arguments on which the budget hard-liners rely to make their case. A realistic reappraisal will surely assign budget cuts a more modest role in the battle against inflation.

Under the somewhat incendiary heading of "myths," let me examine some of the misapprehensions, dubious assumptions, and questionable assertions that seem to underlie the zeal of the budgetcutters. To them, the term "myth" may he a red flag. But it saves space and may serve to organize the mind.

Myth number one: Profligate budget expansion has plunged us into this inflation.

Part of the answer to this myth is well known: skyrocketing food, fuel, and commodity prices, coupled with excessive dollar devaluation, accounted for the great bulk of our 1973–74 inflation. Though excess demand compounded the problem in 1973, inflation even then was as much a supply-squeeze and cost-push phenomenon as it was a product of demand-pull. Today, it is rapidly maturing into a self-propelling price-wage spiral.

Less well known, perhaps, is that recent real budget increases are being held to modest levels: the *real* volume of total federal spending (in constant dollars) is somewhat *lower* today than it was at the end of 1972.

Two perspectives on the "huge" $30 billion spending increase (to $305 billion) in the current year's budget also cut it down to size:

- In high-employment terms, revenues are rising $33 billion this year. Indeed, with normal economic growth plus inflation of only 5 percent a year, federal revenue increases between now and 1980 would average $44 billion a year, according to Brookings projections.
- Of the $30 billion budget increase this year, $19 billion is mandated under open-ended programs, and another $7 billion is earmarked for boosts in defense and federal pay, leaving only $4 billion for "relatively discretionary domestic programs." Only a 2 percent increase, far less than the rate of inflation, is projected for social grant programs.

Myth number two: Huge federal deficits have poured fuel on the fires of inflation.

That surely was a valid view in the Vietnam inflation, but just as surely is *not* the case in the 1973–74 inflation.

On the contrary. After being very stimulative in 1972, the budget came hard about in 1973–74. Measured in terms of a high-employment economy (and regardless of the requiems being sung for the high-employment budget concept, it remains the best shorthand measure of the budget's economic impact) the budget turned from a $2 billion deficit in fiscal 1973 to a $10 billion surplus in fiscal 1974. And it's heading for a surplus of over $15 billion (annual rate) in the first half of calendar 1975. Even if one prefers to use 4½ percent rather than 4 percent as a measure of high employment, the *shift* toward restraint—and it is the *shift* that counts most in the impact on aggregate demand—would still be over $15 billion.

On a national income accounts (NIA) basis, the *actual* federal budget deficit has also been shrinking steadily: from $20 billion in fiscal 1972, to $15 billion in 1973, to less than $2 billion in fiscal 1974. Indeed, the NIA budget was in balance by mid-1974.

Granted, a surplus in 1973 would have been even better. But the key point is that even after adjusting for the revenue-boosting impact of inflation, federal fiscal policy *has* been leaning against the inflationary wind.

Myth number three: When one adds back into the budget the net borrowings of "de-budgeted" agencies (federally sponsored agencies like Fannie Mae and the Home Loan Banks and wholly owned agencies like the Ex-Im Bank and the Postal Service), the "total" federal deficit last year was not $3.5 billion but $21 billion.

But that surely mixes oranges with apples. The Commerce Department quite rightly excludes the credit operations even of the on-budget agencies from its national income account calculations of the federal budget. Why? Because they represent the trading of one asset (cash) for another asset (debt obligations) rather than the purchase of goods and services or transfers of purchasing power.

Federal off-budget credit operations are an important part of total U.S. financial flows—federal agency securities represented 31 percent of the net increase in all money and capital market securities in 1973. It is obviously desirable to coordinate their borrowing and lending activities with Federal Reserve policy. And the net impact of their credit operations—along with those of thrift institutions and others—must be weighed in formulating U.S. fiscal policy.

But in effect to single out one set of lenders like FHMA and FHLB and imply that *their* net lending should be matched with increased taxes runs counter to economic logic. Would the advocates of this position have us boost taxes by, say, $15 billion to match their net lending this year and then, if there were a net repayment of $10 billion next year, cut taxes by $25 billion at that time?

Indeed, if one is going to play the budget consolidation game, it would be a good deal less illogical to combine state-local budgets with the federal budget. This consolidated budget shows an *actual* surplus of nearly $4 billion in 1973. I say "less illogical," because recent state-local surpluses are directly related to rapidly growing federal grants that help generate federal deficits. But I do not press the point (since state-local budgets are part of the "rest of the world" for purposes of setting federal fiscal policy targets).

Myth number four: Cutting the budget offers us so much anti-inflationary clout that we should move ahead on it and make fiscal policy even more restrictive than it is.

A variety of econometric studies have all come to the same conclusion on this subject: short of brutal budget-slashing, budget cuts do not offer much in the way of relief from inflation. The University of Michigan and the Data Resources models—as well as studies cited by OMB Director Roy Ash last June—all conclude that cutting federal spending by $5 billion would shave only one tenth of one percent or less off of the rate of inflation. In exchange for this negligible benefit, the cost would be in the range of 100,000 to 200,000 jobs.

Myth number five: Since budget-cutting would give the economy a psychological uplift, it would cost far less in lost jobs and lost output than the models indicate.

Nothing we know on the basis of common-sense economic analysis or past evidence supports the assertion that cutting the budget will generate a sudden surge of confidence in the stock market and other financial markets, and that the resulting contagion will invigorate rather than subdue the economy. What a budget cut *may* do is to free funds for use in credit-hungry private markets. That indirect effect, not any psychological impact, might provide some offset to the direct demand-weakening effect of the cut.

Myth number six: In the face of raging inflation, budget policy has to be a one-way street, namely, cut, cut, cut. The main contribution the federal government can make to the battle against inflation is to tighten its own belt.

This view fails to recognize that a comprehensive budget policy for "fighting inflation" has to embrace measures to compensate the low and moderate income groups who are bearing the brunt of both inflation and recession. This requires bigger outlays for public service jobs, unemployment compensation, job training, food stamp and housing allowances, and the like. It calls for payroll tax and income tax relief for the working poor and those of moderate incomes.

In other words, the resources freed by pruning unneeded or wasteful expenditures from the budget—and by removing oil and other tax shelters—can find ready and responsible outlets in redressing the grievances of those groups (and industries like housing) that have been ground under the hobnailed boots of inflation and monetary-fiscal austerity.

In passing, one should note that a number of summiteers, especially in the business and financial community, seem to support a different version of budget offsets. They wave the balanced-budget banner and urge expenditure cuts, yet in the next breath press for larger "tax expenditures" in the form of tax cuts on investment income, capital gains, savings, capital spending, and so on. Economic summitry is hardly synonymous with economic symmetry.

Myth number seven: Surely, out of this year's $305–310 billion budget, one can readily find savings of $5 to $10 billion, a mere 2% or 3% cut.

Granted, many programs are marbled with fat that makes them juicier and tastier without making them more nourishing. Granted also, some savings can be achieved in the process of shifting budget priorities. But even with its improved procedures and staff, Congress will find this a slow and painstaking job.

Quite apart from its depressing effect on a sagging economy, a crash program to cut the current budget "below $300 billion" when we are already one-quarter into the fiscal year is likely to be disruptive and inefficient. It will focus on those programs that the government can get its hands on quickly rather than those that are wasteful and of low priority. Equity and efficiency will be poorly served.

Myth number eight: Nonetheless, since we must balance the budget in fiscal 1976 and develop surpluses thereafter, it is imperative to get started on budget-cutting now.

A balanced budget *could* be the right economic policy for fiscal 1976 only if (a) the economy is well on its way to full employment by then and (b) the Federal Reserve can be relied upon to balance overly tight fiscal policy with an easing of monetary policy. But if these conditions are not satisfied, a balanced Bicentennial budget will be a will-o'-the wisp—budget cuts that retard recovery and the expansion of tax revenues that goes with it would prove to be self-defeating.

But what of the federal surpluses we will need later in the 1970's to irrigate the capital markets, to help finance the huge capital outlays we will need to meet our energy needs, expand capacity, and apply the latest technology? The requisites of noninflationary capital spending, as now projected, clearly call for those surpluses. But they do not, of themselves, call for budget cuts.

The Brookings projections already cited indicate that revenues will grow so rapidly that even with only moderate restraint on the expenditure side, the federal budget could generate large surpluses. Given present budget initiatives and using a modest inflation factor of only 3 percent, these projections show a $39 billion net high-employment surplus by 1980.

Myth number nine: When all is said and done, the fact is that the 1969–71 "economic game plan"–the lineal ancestor of today's "old-time religion"–was subduing infla-

tion even before Mr. Nixon slapped on the wage-price freeze. Inflation had already receded from the 6 percent-plus level in 1970 "to the 3½–4 percent zone by the first half of 1971."

Neither the conclusion nor the numbers stand up under close analysis. Since the alleged effectiveness of fiscal-monetary restraint in 1971 is so central to the argument for budgetary austerity today, it is important to demonstrate how misleading it is:

• Although the rise in the Consumer Price Index slowed down from 6 percent in 1969–70 to 4½ percent by mid-1971, two-thirds of that improvement was simply a swing in mortgage interest rates, up 10 percent in 1969–70 and down 11 percent by mid-1971. Commodities other than food kept rising at about a 4 percent rate throughout the period.

• The wholesale price index showed little change, rising 3.7 percent from 1969 to 1970 and 3.5 percent from mid-1970 to mid-1971.

• The consumption component of the GNP deflator rose 4.8 percent in 1969–70 and 4.4 percent from spring 1970 to spring 1971, with prices of consumer services and durable goods actually rising.

• The "chain price index for gross private product," perhaps the best comprehensive index of quarterly price movements, rose 4.8 percent (annual rate) during the second quarter of 1971, actually a bit more than the 1969–70 increase.

• The weight of the evidence led Arthur Burns to conclude in his statement to the Joint Economic Committee in July 1971 that substantial progress had *not* been made in checking inflation.

The foregoing effort to separate fact from fiction on the budget is not designed to shield the budget from its fair share of belt-tightening and waste-cutting in the face of virulent inflation. Rather, it seeks to reduce the twin dangers that we will vent our inflationary frustrations in unwise and unwarranted budget cuts and let the zeal for fiscal restraint block the tax and budget relief so urgently needed to temper the wind to the shorn lambs.

Although the economy was sinking into the worst recession since the Great Depression of the 1930's, President Ford came forward with a post-summit "first stage program" almost exclusively preoccupied with inflation. In its one-dimensional focus, it was of a piece with the old-time religion of Nixonomics—if anything, a bit more Catholic than the (deposed) Pope.

Yet, finding the new candor, openness, and civility of the Ford White House such a welcome relief after the Nixon Administration, one shied away from carping criticism and resolved doubts in the President's favor. In that spirit, the following appraisal seeks to find some kernels of comfort in the Ford program before turning to its obvious deficiencies.

One should note that the Congress—specifically, the House Ways and Means Committee, where revenue legislation originates—had not waited for the President but had gone to work on a tax measure that included some structural changes and a very modest program for tax relief for lower income groups.

The Ford Program and Recession

THE WALL STREET JOURNAL *October 8, 1974*

It isn't that there is so much to be said *against* Mr. Ford's unbold new program. It's just that there isn't much to be said *for* it.

One has to hope that Mr. Ford's modest moves are merely a down payment on bigger and better things to come. Several of his initiatives fall in this category of small steps in the right direction, even though they have a certain "yes, but" quality.

First, broadening the policy perspective on inflation, as he proposes, to include low-income tax relief, public employment, and bigger jobless benefits is a distinct plus. But protecting the poor, the near-poor, and the jobless from the inroads of inflation and the ravages of recession will require far more than a scant $2 billion of tax relief, the funding of 83,000 Community Improvement jobs, and special unemployment compensation.

Second, his willingness to bell the higher-income cats with a 5 percent surtax recognizes that inflation's inequity is a two-sided coin. But given the huge tax bounties now enjoyed by the oil industry and by the well-to-do users of countless tax shelters, it would seem that the 5 percent surtax—at least on individuals—is belling the wrong cats. The temporary 5 percent surtax, if needed at all, would make sense only as earnest money on a rigorous permanent tax reform.

Third, it is encouraging to see that Mr. Ford is now giving higher priority to cutbacks in demand for energy, and especially for oil. But one must hope that he is prepared to call for greater sacrifices at home and greater cooperation abroad to achieve a balanced energy budget at lower levels of consumption and lowered OPEC oil prices.

Fourth, Mr. Ford's challenging of government-sanctioned restrictive practices and regulatory procedures that prop up costs and prices merits warm applause. But two provisos: One, that the sacred cows, once rounded up and branded, actually be led to slaughter. Two, that the slaughter not be carried to the point of letting the consumer and the environment fend for themselves. It will take heroic efforts in the public interest to prevent perversion of this initiative by powerful private interests.

Fifth, as part of a balanced program, it makes sense to increase the investment credit to facilitate capital spending. But he proposes only a one-year corporate surtax yielding $2.1 billion to match a permanent increase in the credit giving corporations $2.7 billion a year from now on. That is, at best, a curious kind of "balance."

Finally, it is all well and good to call for federal budget belt-tightening, *provided* that the fat cut out of the existing budget is used to put some muscle into programs to help the workers, consumers, and taxpayers hardest hit by inflation and recession.

So the Ford program—partly by endorsing moves already afoot like the hodge-podge tax package coming out of the Ways and Means Committee and partly by its own initiatives like the 5 percent surtax and 10 percent investment credit—seeks to carve out some new beachheads in the war on inflation. But unless and until those beachheads are enlarged, the program still boils down to monetary-fiscal austerity. In its heart, it still knows the "old-time religion" is right.

One test of this appraisal is to run the Ford program through the forecasting models, as several forecasters have done. The resulting change in projected GNP and inflation for the next three quarters: negligible.

For whatever reason—economic conviction, political "realism," or unresolved conflicts in the White House—Mr. Ford's first-stage program does not come to grips with either the special nature of today's inflation or the lengthening shadows of recession.

Anti-inflation policy should be tailored to take account of two distinguishing characteristics of the 1973–75 inflation:

- One, while economic policy is still busy fighting excess-demand inflation, we are actually suffering from a witches' brew of commodity inflation that is now turning into a full-fledged price-wage spiral. Both of these types of inflationary virus are highly resistant to monetary-fiscal antibiotics.
- Two, in most U.S. inflations "one person's price is another's income," so that in spite of some reshuffling, there is no net loss in real income. Not so in 1973–75. Commodity inflation has transferred tens of billions of dollars of *real* income out of the pockets of urban consumers and wage-earners into the hands of farmers and

foreigners—where it is beyond the reach of the collective bargaining process. If the wage "catch-up" process now succeeds in recouping the *full* rise in cost-of-living, it will only serve to push up prices in another self-defeating round of inflation.

These special characteristics of inflation suggest four lessons for policy:

- While maintaining monetary and fiscal restraint and appealing for consumer and business restraint in food and energy consumption, Mr. Ford left a gaping hole in his program by failing to call for effective measures to induce wage and price restraint.
- Payroll tax and income tax relief could relieve some of the real income squeeze on workers and reduce wage pressures.
- Any tax relief should be tilted toward the lower income groups who are the hardest hit by the losses of real income and have the weakest defenses against them.
- To superimpose on the real losses of 1973–75 inflation the further losses of a severe recession will put the consumer in double jeopardy and intensify the struggle of the strong to recoup their losses at the expense of the weak.

This brings us to the second glaring omission of the Ford program: it is still fighting largely a one-front war against inflation, leaving the soft underbelly of a deepening recession largely unguarded. Yet that recession exposes the economy not just to losses of jobs, output, and profit, but to erosion of the productivity and capital expansion on which our long-run defenses against inflation rest.

We are now nine months into a peculiar but all-too-genuine recession. Never before in modern history have U.S. monetary-fiscal controls still been locked into a "choke-off-demand" position this far along in a slump. And the worst is yet to come.

A careful reappraisal of the GNP outlook just completed

by my colleague, George Perry of Brookings, leads us to the glum conclusions that the economic slide is worsening; that unemployment will rise above 7 percent by mid-1975; that in the absence of early and decisive easing of policy by the Federal Reserve and the White House, there is no prospect for economic recovery before the second half of 1975.

Since our expectations are at the blue end (but not off the deep end) of the forecasting spectrum, it may be useful to consider briefly the challenges encountered on the more pessimistic phases of the forecast.

Consumption: Why do we expect a continued lackluster performance by consumers in the face of their recent robust saving rate of 8 percent? That high rate reflects mainly last year's surge in farm income and this year's slump in auto sales: adjusting the saving rate for these two factors shrinks it to less than 6½ percent. Consumers have in fact been scrambling to keep up with higher prices, not building up reserves of buying power.

Inventories: The rate of accumulation of business inventories, even after removing the huge swing in autos, dropped sharply substantially in the first half of 1974. Why do we think it will drop still farther? First, the accumulation rate throughout this period was far above the sustainable long-term rate. Second, it resulted in the sharpest upsurge in the ratio of inventories to total final sales since the Korean War. Third, as shortages ease, businesses will pull inventory levels back into line with final sales. In the process, production for inventory will plummet in the next six to nine months.

Housing: How do we justify our forecast of less than one million starts? The inroads of costly and scarce mortgage money will take a heavy toll—they are already reflected in a big drop in new housing permits.

Unemployment: Since unemployment confounded the experts by rising so slowly until the bounce to 5.8 percent in September, why do we expect it to climb above 7 percent? After all, it rose far less than expected in the face of a severe drop in real output during the first half of 1974. Perhaps firms accepted White House assurances that they were merely passing through a brief "energy spasm" or "phantom recession" that would soon be reversed. Also, rising profits—bolstered by inventory gains—obscured growing signs of weakness. And labor force growth slowed to a walk. But now, with prospects of early recovery vanishing, profits eroding, and labor force growth picking up, unemployment is returning to a more normal relationship with output—and that spells over 7 percent unemployment.

There is no mystery about the policy inferences to be drawn from the foregoing appraisal. One can only hope that Mr. Ford's next move will be to step gently but firmly on the wage-price brakes and let up moderately but promptly on the fiscal-monetary brakes.

Having complimented Mr. Burns on the Fed's loosening of the monetary screw, Mr. Ford should now remind him that one good turn deserves another. Without throwing restraint to the winds, the Fed should release more oxygen to the housing industry, financial markets, public utilities, and small businesses that are still gasping for relief.

With economic activity sliding farther and farther below economic potential, Mr. Ford can now afford to couple responsive humanitarian policy with responsible fiscal policy in a program of *net* tax and budget relief in the range of $6–8 billion for the victims of inflation. A $1,400 billion economy with growing reserves of idle machines and workers can put that offering to good use in expanding jobs and output without much more than an inflationary hiccup.

The strategic retreat from excessive monetary-fiscal tightness should be accompanied by a solid advance on the wage-price front. Mr. Ford should move to equip his Council on Wage and Price Stability with enough clout to deal firmly with big business and powerful unions that flout the public interest. Granted, labor and business are sour on controls, especially after the fiasco of Phases 3 and 4. But it is hard to believe that consumers will put up with the alternative of deep recession and unchecked cost-push. It would be a far better thing to develop effective wage-price restraint now than be pushed into a new freeze and rigid controls in the future.

It is important to recognize the interplay, indeed the synergism, between monetary-fiscal easing and wage-price tightening. On one hand, the latter enlarges the elbow room for the former. Holding prices and wages in check in the noncompetitive and demi-competitive segments of labor and product markets reduces the inflationary content of any given tax cut or spending increase in a slack economy.

On the other hand, income and payroll tax cuts applied with skill and statesmanship can do double duty, not only righting some of the wrongs of inflation but becoming part of a social contract in which real income losses of wage earners that cannot be recaptured in the bargaining process are consciously restored through the (un)taxing process.

To avoid misunderstanding, let me add two comments. First, the consensus forecast today may be less bleak than ours, but it fully justifies a decidedly less austere fiscal and monetary stance. For it foresees essentially a flat economy well into 1975, unemployment of at least 6½ percent, and marked increases in unused productive capacity. Second, compared with fiscal-monetary action in previous recessions, the proposed easing is indeed moderate. It would let up on the brakes, not step on the gas.

Mr. Ford's refreshing exposure to the economic facts of life—through both summitry and the new, if chaotic, candor of his advisers—has at least and at last moved policy off dead center. Now one has to hope that his continued exposure, not just to the unrelenting hot winds of inflation, but to the ever-colder winds of recession will lead to a balanced two-front war against these twin enemies.

The skidding economy had quickly consigned President Ford's last-gasp anti-inflation program to the dustbin of economic history. Unemployment shot up from 5.5 percent in August to 7.2 percent in December, industrial production was sinking (see Chart 6), real income was falling, and the consumer was going into hiding. Even the most myopic observer could see that this was a snowballing recession and that inflation was beginning to ease.

The recognition lag had been painfully long and costly. But by January, the policy tide was turning fast. A serious question still remained: Would the White House and Congress now take bold enough action to limit the economic slide and put the economy back on a solid recovery track?

Some excerpts from "The Economy in 1975," my Jan-

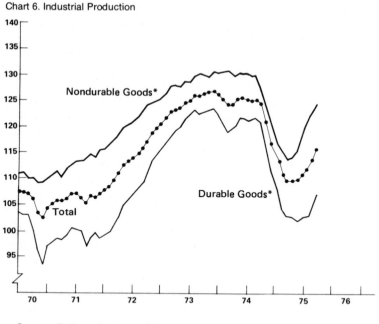

Chart 6. Industrial Production

Source: Federal Reserve Board
*Seasonally Adjusted

uary 15 forecast article in *The Wall Street Journal,*
served to characterize the profound shifts in the economic situation and policy posture and expressed the
fear that anti-recession policy, already too late, might
also be too little.

The Economy in 1975

THE WALL STREET JOURNAL *January 15, 1975*

From the stream of tax proposals now flowing out of the
White House, one can infer that the Ford Administration
has at last got the multiple message that we are in the
midst of a steep slide into recession, calling for a large tax
cut; that boosting oil prices will sterilize still more purchasing power and require an even bigger tax cut; that
with the shock waves of the 1973–74 inflation now subsiding and no excess demand in sight, recession can safely be
attacked as Public Enemy Number One.

So, in a sense, the qualitative battle for sensible economic policy is being won. But the quantitative battle is
only now being joined. How sharply we should cut taxes
and ease money depends in large part on how deep and
stubborn a recession we face and how far and fast inflation
will ebb. . . .

Policy has already waited too long to avoid the deepest
recession since the Great Depression. Still at stake is, first,
the margin by which the current recession earns that dubious award; second, the timing of the turn from recession
to recovery; and, third, how many years it will take us to
get back within striking distance of reasonably full employment (say, 5 percent unemployment). It is worth noting that if recovery started next fall and proceeded at a
sustained 6 percent annual growth rate in real GNP, it
would not bring us back even to 6 percent unemployment
before late 1978 . . .

Real GNP will shrink in 1975 for the second year in a

row—the first back-to-back declines since just after World War II. Following a 2 percent year-over-year drop in 1974, real GNP will fall another 3 percent this year. . . .

The most heartening aspect of the 1975 economic picture is the prospect of progressive relief from the traumatic price pressures of 1973–74. Raw materials prices are falling world-wide. With the whole world economy in recession, they should continue to soften throughout the year. . . . U.S. inflation should drop from its 10 to 15 percent rates of 1974 to the neighborhood of 5 percent before the year is out. Without new policy blunders or crop failures, and given appropriately stimulative policy, we could expect 1976 to bring solid economic recovery coupled with inflation rates below 5 percent.

Against this backdrop of a sagging economy, receding inflation, and cold downdrafts from fiscal-monetary and energy policies, the case for easier Federal Reserve policies and a prompt and bold tax cut is overwhelming. We need to restore the health of the U.S. economy for its own sake. And we must be ever mindful that as we slide deeper into recession, we not only undermine the ability of our trading partners to cope with their oil-cum-recession crises but dangerously increase economic pressures on the Third World.

The right medicine now for recession and unemployment without triggering unwanted side effects on inflation would be a well-structured tax cut of $20 to $25 billion. . . .

The greatest enemy of a tax cut of this size today is what one might call "fiscal acrophobia," an unreasoning fear of fiscal heights. A $20 to $25 billion tax cut sounds high until one puts it into today's rather than yesterday's fiscal and economic perspectives:

- It would do no more than offset the "inflation drag," that is, the automatic increase in effective federal income tax rates "legislated" by inflation in 1973–75.
- It would offset only about half of the prospective 1975 "oil drag," the combination of quadrupled crude oil

prices plus the price effects of new oil policies now fore-shadowed.

- It would equal less than two-thirds of a year's automatic growth in federal tax revenues which, at present tax rates, runs close to $35 billion a year.
- It would be only 1½ percent of the projected GNP for 1975.
- It would be smaller than the 1964 federal income tax cut translated into today's terms. That $11 billion cut would be $26 billion today. Yet it was enacted when GNP was running 7 percent below the U.S. economic potential calculated at 4 percent unemployment, while GNP in 1975 will soon be running 10 percent below our economic potential calculated at 5 percent unemployment.

It is not an exaggeration to say that the biggest danger to the economy in 1975 is that we will think too small. Given what is now at stake in both economic and human terms, in both domestic and international terms—and given that inflation forces are ebbing, that excess demand is years away, and that tax cuts will help reduce cost-push pressures—our policymakers cannot afford *not* to think big.

Because the recession was gathering momentum so fast, President Ford unfolded his economic program in the State of the Union Message and a special energy message well before sending his Budget and Economic Messages to Congress in early February. Profound as the change in his policy stance may have been, it still reflected considerable "fiscal acrophobia":

- Instead of a $20 to $25 billion tax cut, he proposed "an immediate one-year tax cut of $16 billion," consisting of a $12 billion rebate on 1974 taxes and a $4 billion investment tax credit for business.
- Simultaneously, he asked Congress to "pare $17 billion from the fiscal 1976 budget."

- On the energy front, Ford's approach was reflected in his statement that "the only practical and effective way to achieve energy independence . . . is by allowing prices of oil and gas to move higher—high enough to discourage consumption and encourage the exploration and development of new energy sources." To serve this end, he proposed an extraordinary energy package seeking to balance $30 billion of energy taxes with $30 billion of "energy tax offsets," as follows:

- The energy taxes were to take the form of $9.5 billion in import and excise taxes on crude oil; $8.5 billion of excise taxes on natural gas; and $12 billion of "windfall profits taxes" in the form of a graduated excise tax on the sale of domestic crude oil.
- The energy tax offsets were to be in the form of a $16.5 billion cut in individual income taxes; a $6.5 billion cut in corporate income taxes; and $7 billion of federal payments "to compensate nontaxpayers, state and local governments, and federal agencies for higher energy costs."

Simultaneously, of course, crude oil prices were to be controlled. All in all, it was indeed a remarkable program—with little chance of enactment. Critics were quick to label it "Gerry built" and to characterize it as "the Ford giveth, and the Ford taketh away." Most economists felt that while it was desirable to rely mainly on the market pricing system in the longer run for these purposes, the Ford program for abrupt decontrol and rapid energy price run-ups would worsen both recession and inflation in the short run. In spite of its neatly balanced 30–30 appearance, the program would have raised energy prices (including coal and other competing sources) by over $40 billion, while the cushioning offsets in terms of consumer prices and purchasing power would have been only about $25 billion. Hence, in the process of using the price mechanism to curb energy use and boost production, it would have given another fillip to inflation and put a sizable crimp in effective consumer buying power.

It was against this background that the House Ways

and Means Committee—which had been expanded and "liberalized" after the sweeping Democratic gains in the 1974 Congressional elections—went into high gear on antirecession tax action. As they did so, all indications were that the Congress would enlarge the President's tax cuts to fight recession and drastically alter the President's energy tax program—or simply postpone action in that field.

To aid it in its urgent but vexed deliberations, the Ways and Means Committee called on a number of outside witnesses to make proposals in both the antirecession and energy tax fields. On January 28, I made the following statement to the Committee.

Tax Actions to Combat Recession and Conserve Energy

With the cascade of advice, analysis, and statistics pouring in on the House Ways and Means Committee, it is not easy to know what one can add that might be helpful in coping with an inflation-ridden and energy-bedeviled recession. But perhaps it would be useful to look at (a) the three basic forces that have propelled us into this worst recession since the Great Depression and (b) the policy actions, especially those within the jurisdiction of this Committee, that could pull us out.

The 1975 economy is reeling under the impact of three heavy blows: monetary overkill, fiscal overkill, and the debilitating eruption of oil prices.

MONETARY POLICY

The first and most obvious blow is an unduly prolonged period of super-tight money. However understandable the Federal Reserve's motivation may be (in terms of curbing not only inflation but the inventory binge of early 1974), its decision to put the economy back on a starvation monetary diet after the recession had already begun—and then holding it relentlessly on that diet while the recession progressed in 1974—has been a major factor in strangulation of the economy.

The remedy is clear: The Federal Reserve System should at long last recognize that recession is now Public Enemy Number One and redirect its fire accordingly. Grudging and reluctant easing of money is not enough. Militant and aggressive ease is required to reverse the recession and revive the economy.

FISCAL POLICY

A second and less visible, but equally deadly, recessionary force has been one of more direct import to this Committee, namely, the dramatic tightening of fiscal policy in 1973–74. Although masked by the shrinking revenues and resulting deficits growing out of recession, the federal budget has actually been making a massive shift from stimulus to restriction.

- In the very teeth of our slide into recession, the federal budget has made roughly a $24 billion swing toward restriction in less than 18 months. Instead of taking a hypothetical full-employment level, one can start with the trough level of 4.6 percent unemployment in the second quarter of 1973, when the federal budget was running at a $7 billion deficit rate (NIA basis). If the jobless rate had held at 4.6 percent, the federal deficit would have turned into a $27 billion surplus by the third quarter of 1974. After subtracting $10 billion to allow for the nonrecurring corporate tax revenues arising from temporarily bloated inventory profits, one is left with a $24 billion shift in five quarters.
- This shift is continuing and would tighten the fiscal noose by another $15 billion in the first half of 1975.
- Indeed, in the unlikely event that Mr. Ford's tax rebate plan would be the only tax action taken, the full-

employment surplus would be back above $25 billion by the middle of 1975.

In other words, while we are shivering from the cold blasts of a thirteen-month-old recession, the fiscal and monetary dials are still set to fight the hot blasts of inflation and boom. Small wonder that the slippery slope of recession is so steep.

Without going into any detailed prescription, I believe that the severe economic and fiscal crunch and its devastating impact on lower income groups strongly suggest certain guidelines for quick tax action:

- Leaving aside the boost in the investment credit (some form of which seems highly desirable), I would urge the Committee to adopt the substance of Mr. Ford's $12 billion shot-in-the-arm for the economy, but not its form. For both humanitarian and economic reasons, it should be heavily concentrated in the lower and lower-middle income groups. Indeed, for maximum equity and economic impact, it ought to embrace people too poor to pay income taxes, much on the pattern of the President's proposal to give a flat payment—a kind of "negative income tax"—to persons in this category. And for maximum effect, it should be paid all at once and as soon as humanly possible.

- The one-shot quickie cut is obviously not enough. If that were to be the only net tax cut, the economy might well sag back into recession in 1976. What is needed is a major *net* continuing cut of perhaps $20 to $25 billion so that we will not only *get* but *keep* the economy moving again.

- President Ford's tax cut proposals for the longer run (in his 30–30 energy program), including increases in exemptions and low income allowances and cutting the first bracket rate in half, suggest the right tone and pattern for the bulk of the short-run cut.

- If the precise formulation of the continuing cut is so difficult and time-consuming that it would delay action unduly, the Committee should consider coupling with its one-shot rebate action and immediate reduction of, say, two percentage points in the withholding rate (together with a higher cutoff level of withholding), leaving the precise configuration of rates and exemptions for a follow-up bill. The follow-up bill might also take up some key reform provisions.

- This streamlined approach would facilitate quick action, an immediate $12 billion injection, and continuing tax therapy that would fatten pay envelopes at the rate of $10 to $15 billion a year. The more deliberate follow-up bill could fill in the details and enlarge the cut in final liabilities.

I need not dwell on the well-established fact that, with inflation ebbing and the economy operating more than 10 percent below its $1.5 billion-plus potential by mid-year, the proposed tax cut is (a) modest and (b) noninflationary.

THE OIL DRAG AND TAX POLICY

The third repressive force on the U.S. and indeed the world economy is the tremendous tribute we are paying the oil potentates and royalty collectors. The quadrupling of prices by the OPEC countries is now siphoning some $30 billion a year out of consumers' pockets, with only a trickle coming back into the U.S. economy in the form of higher investment and demand for U.S. exports. While *de*flating demand by $30 billion a year, it has *in*flated costs and prices, adding about three percentage points to our rate of inflation.

President Ford's 30–30 energy program would deal a fourth blow to the economy—another double whammy that would boost inflation and worsen recession. Without the Ford program, the inflation rate is heading toward a manageable though still high rate of 5 percent by a year from now. But the President's taxes on oil and natural gas would boost the inflation rate, as measured by the rise in the Consumer Price Index, by over 50 percent—to a rate of 8 percent in the first half of 1976.

The further recessionary blow would arise from the $30 billion add-on to crude oil and natural gas costs, to which mark-ups would undoubtedly add several billion more by the time the consumer pays the bill. The offsetting action under the President's program would bolster consumer buying power by perhaps $10 billion less than the increased bill for oil and gas. This would subdue rather than stimulate the economy.

Everyone recognizes that the solution to our energy problem is a choice among evils. Given the damaging effects of the President's 30–30 program on the nation's efforts to stem inflation and stimulate economic recovery, I urge the Committee to consider a combination of oil import quotas and allocations, gasoline rationing, and a stair-step increase in the gasoline excise tax. The basic contours and rationale of this program would be as follows:

- The gasoline tax would be phased in, perhaps starting in 1976, at the rate of 10 cents per gallon per year, imposed in quarterly steps of 2½ cents each. The ultimate level of the tax could be set at a minimum of 30 cents a gallon, leaving open the question of whether a further increase would be necessary or desirable.

- Your Committee and the Congress would want to develop an offset to the tax, to be phased in with it. This could be in the form of a refundable tax credit, though some of the revenues could well be reserved for the development of alternative energy sources.

- The stair-step introduction of the tax would be vastly superior to hitting the economy with a huge new oil price shock all at once. The tax would gradually move up as the economy and incomes are moving up and as inflation wanes. And the programing of the tax and spending offsets could be more deliberate and precise.

- The particular merit of the stair-step tax in relation to rationing would be this: It would speed up the takeover by the market pricing system from the rationing system. By progressively curbing demand through the steadily rising price (with supplies meanwhile responding to the lofty price of "new" oil), a market clearing intersect of supply and demand would be reached much sooner than without the tax. In fact, with a "white rationing" system in which ration coupons could be sold on the open market, the declining price of the coupons would be a guide to the date of termination of rationing.

- A further advantage of the gradual phasing in of the gasoline tax is that both consumers and producers of automobiles could make more gradual adjustments to smaller and more gasoline-efficient cars rather than suffering the more disruptive and costly impact of a one-time jump.

There is cause for encouragement that the White House has faced up to both the economic and energy problems in a resolute way and has proposed bold action. There is cause for concern that the President and his advisers are not showing the spirit of compromise and conciliation required to hammer out a better program with maximum speed. There is cause for optimism that this Committee and the Congress are accepting the President's call to action and undertaking to re-shape the program in a way that will strike the best balance in fighting recession and curbing energy use without reigniting inflation.

Working at long last with White House blessing—and prodding—the Congress moved swiftly on the antirecession tax program. Each new statistic and each new hearing underscored the need for a large and speedy tax cut. Both in open hearings and in behind-the-scenes briefing sessions with key Senators and Representatives, economists played an important role in getting Congress to raise its sights. From initial and abortive moves toward a $5 or $6 billion tax cut program during most of 1974, the targets began to escalate as some

Senators talked of a $10–12 billion program late in 1974. The President entered the bidding in January with his $16 billion cut. But by February—after being assured by leading economists that the still-plunging economy could readily absorb tax cuts of $25 or $30 billion (in a few cases, even $35 billion) without rekindling inflation—the Congress had clearly been conditioned to thinking of cuts in the $20 to $30 billion range. By early March, the House had sent to the Senate a bill calling for tax cuts of $21 billion while the Joint Economic Committee was calling for a one-shot rebate of $8 billion and a continuing cut of $24 billion.

The hurry-up tax cut process in early 1975 was the occasion for one of those exercises in political irony to which the U.S. system of divided powers lends itself. A by-then thoroughly alarmed President—who as a Congressman had never witnessed passage of a major tax measure in less than six months—urged lightning speed on the tax cut and berated Congress for the unnecessary delays that were jeopardizing the prospects of recovering from the dreadful recession.

These charges were directed at a Democratic Congress that had been virtually hooted down for its timely efforts to mount a modest fiscal offensive against the gathering forces of recession in 1974. The liberal Democrats who had led the way lost political points for allegedly being soft on inflation rather than winning plaudits for spotting the recession and proposing modest tax cuts to do double duty in countering the downswing and giving some relief to those hit hardest by losses of real income in inflation and jobs in recession.

Ironic also was the President's insistence that the deficit line for fiscal 1976 should be held strictly at $60 billion lest further sins of inflation be visited on us all. The irony lay both in the widely recognized (and not unprecedented) budgetary legerdemain—in the form of overstated receipts (e.g., on offshore oil leases) and spending cutbacks that no Congress would accept—and in the adamant position that the deficit constraint allowed $16 billion of tax cuts and no more.

The battle of the deficit was in full swing as the tax bill reached the Senate and the following article was written.

Deficit: Where Is Thy Sting?

THE WALL STREET JOURNAL *March 7, 1975*

As the Senate tackles tax cuts to fight recession and the Congress considers budget relief to succor the victims of inflation and unemployment, the legislators are being bombarded with dire warnings that the resulting deficits will crowd out private borrowing, push up interest rates, and rekindle inflation. Lest they be unduly inhibited or even intimidated by this barrage of scare-talk about unmanageable and inflationary deficits, let them bear in mind four central facts.

First, the very forces of rampant recession that make tax and budgetary stimulus so imperative are the forces that open up a yawning financial gap for the deficit to fill. The deeper the plunge of the economy, the greater the shrinkage of private outlets for savings in the form of corporate borrowing, mortgages, and consumer installment debts. In an economy running $175 billion below its potential, the deficit will help fill the void, not elbow out private borrowing.

Second, for clear thinking, the Congress and the country should divide budget deficits into two parts:

- Type A, the passive deficits generated by the negative effects of recession and slack on the budget.
- Type B, the active deficits generated by positive fiscal actions—tax cuts and budget boosts—to combat recession and take up economic slack.

The President's Budget is referring to Type A deficits when it says "If the economy were to be as fully employed in 1976 as it was in 1974, we would have $40 billion in additional tax receipts, assuming no change in tax rates, and

$12.7 billion less in aid to the unemployed." This $53 billion is the mirror image of the deficit in output and jobs.

The quickest way to shrink and eventually end such Type A deficits is to incur Type B deficits via swift and bold tax cuts and budget hikes that will get the economy expanding again. Indeed, while such fiscal stimulus will temporarily enlarge the deficit—to perhaps $70 billion in fiscal 1976—it will also pay such large dividends in rapidly rising revenues that it will produce a smaller aggregate deficit for the seventies than would a more timid program.

Third, Congress can and should look to the Federal Reserve to accommodate the large deficit just as it has in past economic slumps. The White House clearly does so, as this passage from the President's *Ecomomic Report* makes clear:

> One way of preventing significant displacement of private investment in a substantially underemployed economy would be to increase the rate of money supply growth to reduce Federal financing pressures. Under such conditions, an increase in monetary growth need not be inflationary in the short run, especially if there is a large unsatisfied demand for liquidity.

In other words, in an economy that has fallen so far from the grace of full employment, the Fed can safely generate the bank reserves and expanding money supply required to ward off rising interest rates and crowding out of private borrowers. And having provided liquidity for today's dehydrated economy, it will have plenty of time to sop up any excess funds before the economy again nears the inflationary danger zone of full employment.

Fourth, just as the swift slide into deep recession makes the return to high-pressure prosperity a distant prospect, so the rapidly dwindling price pressures make a resurgence of inflation a remote threat. In the face of a $175 billion shortfall of aggregate demand, falling commodity prices, and the massive unemployment that is defusing a feared wage explosion, the hot blasts of inflation are turning into a warm breeze.

Since the burden of proof that the fiscal problem is manageable has strangely been shifted by the creators of the problem to their critics, let me elaborate on each of the foregoing points.

On the first, namely, that the recession is drying up credit demands in the private sector and thus freeing funds to finance the Treasury deficit, one quickly finds supporting evidence in both the global and sectoral flow-of-funds figures. For example, the most recent Salomon Brothers' analysis shows total net demand for credit shrinking from $185 billion in 1973 to $163 billion in 1975, even with a jump of $31 billion in federal (including agency) borrowing. Total business and household credit demands are estimated to shrink from $150 billion in 1973 to $95 billion in 1975. Bearing in mind that a fully functioning economy in 1975 could have produced a $200 billion supply of credit, one may conclude that a federal deficit considerably larger than $50 billion could be accommodated without unbearable strains in 1975.

The *Morgan Guaranty Survey* for February, after carefully matching shrunken private credit demand and expanded Treasury needs (even if these run to $60 billion in calendar 1975) concludes that "the interplay of steep declines in economic activity and easing monetary policy affords latitude for an orderly matching of the supply and demand for credit during 1975. As this process unfolds, the near-hysterical whoops in some quarters of an impending financial crunch should subside." Amen!

Turning, second, to the salubrious effect of economic expansion on the federal deficit, one should bear in mind the following numbers:

- Under present tax rates and transfer programs, the federal revenues at full employment would run about $20–25 billion ahead of expenditures in 1975.
- For every $10 billion narrowing of the $175 billion GNP gap, federal revenues rise by about $3 billion and transfer payments shrink by about $1 billion—a handsome return on the investment in expansionary fiscal policy.

- The $12 billion tax cut in 1964 (which translates into a
  $26 billion tax cut today) more than paid for itself by
  1965, indeed, had produced enough economic expansion to generate a surplus in the federal budget by mid-
  1965 prior to Vietnam escalation.

On the third point relating not just to the Federal Reserve's unquestioned ability but to its willingness to accommodate a vigorous attack on recession, one can truly
say that the Fed has hardly begun to fight. True, the
plummeting demand for credit has pulled short-term rates
down dramatically. But its efforts to inject funds into the
economy and help stem the tide of recession have been too
feeble to register on the M_1 seismograph in recent months.
The most optimistic reading of this failure is to assume
that the Fed will practice "percentage averaging" and
allow itself at least a spell of the 8–10 percent growth rate
in money supply that ought to be standard procedure in an
economy cursed by the deepest and longest recession
since the Great Depression and blessed by waning inflation.

Just a word to those who feel that all our policy instruments are tilted in an inflationary direction: Rest assured that the Federal Reserve, with its chronic allergy to
inflation reinforced by searing memories of its untimely
expansiveness in 1968 and 1972, will be a trigger-happy
guardian at the gates of inflationary hell as economic recovery takes hold. One is reminded of Chief Justice
Holmes' dictum that "the power to tax is the power to destroy" and Justice Brandeis' rejoinder, "yes, but not while
this court sits." As the Federal Reserve gingerly shifts
from the brake to the accelerator, apprehensive of the inflationary legacy it might leave, it would do well to bear in
mind that "the power to expand the money supply may be
the power to destroy price stability—but not (necessarily)
while the Federal Reserve Board sits."

On the fourth point, the evidence that the inflationary
tide is going out is mounting month by month. As an historical note, one should mention that the Ford energy pro-

gram would have reversed that tide by tacking about three percentage points onto the inflation rate. But the Congress will not let that happen.

In a rather curious switch, White House spokesmen are more pessimistic on inflation forecasts than most private forecasters. Yet, with sensitive commodity prices off nearly 30 percent in the past three months, with food prices destined to drop if crops are normal, with woefully weak labor markets holding average earnings increases below double-digit levels, and with the Consumer Price Index already easing from a record rise (at annual rates) of 14 percent last summer to about 7 percent in January, it is hard to see what will keep inflation from dropping to 5 percent or below in the second half of 1975.

As an added starter, let me bring in a fifth point in the form of a question: Wherein lies monetary prudence and fiscal responsibility? Was it prudent and responsible (a) to press monetary tightness and fiscal toughness to the point of plunging the economy into a near-depression, and (b) to brush aside those of us who sounded recessionary alarums with soothing reassurances that the economic slide was a mere "energy spasm" or "phantom recession," or "sideways waffling"?

The same disciples of "prudence" and "responsibility" who overstayed tightness and overdid toughness are now counseling caution and urging the Congress to think small on tax and budget policy lest it plunge us into financial perdition and inflationary ruin. But the country would pay a heavy price in prolonged stagnation and stubborn deficits if Congress made the mistake of identifying prudence with timidity and fiscal discipline with niggardly tax cuts and budget parsimony.

In short, the Congress can prudently proceed with a strong program to reverse the recession and revive the economy. No fears of unmanageable deficits or imminent inflation need stay its hand. This is not to say that financing the deficit will be simple nor that it will be accomplished without a pinch here and a bind there. But sources ranging from impeccable to unimpeachable seem to agree that, with a responsive Federal Reserve, the huge deficit can be managed at low interest rates, with little displacement of private investment, and without rekindling inflation.

By March 29, the antirecession tax cut became law (even while the energy program continued to languish in Congress). Though it was not the biggest tax reduction ever enacted—the $11 billion 1964 income tax cut would have come to $26 billion in 1975 dollars—it was the fastest both in enactment and in the immediacy of payoff. It was enacted in 2½ months in contrast with the 1964 tax cut, which took 14 months, and the 1968 surtax, which took ten months. And it provided for an outpouring of over $10 billion in cash, plus a $2 billion reduction in withholding, in the first three months after enactment.

In completely revamping the President's program, the Congress moved a long way toward those who sought (1) a bigger tax cut, (2) more help for those hit hardest by inflation and recession, (3) a swifter pay-off, and (4) more sustained economic stimulus:

- *Size:* In contrast with the Ford proposal of a $12 billion tax rebate for individuals and a $4 billion cut for corporations (in the form of an expanded investment credit), the Tax Reduction Act of 1975 provided $20 billion of rebates and tax cuts for individuals and a $4 billion tax cut for corporations (with a $1.7 billion recapture of revenues from large oil firms, mainly by elimination of their percentage depletion allowance).
- *Distribution:* The Congressional program was far more generous to low income families and social insurance recipients than the President's program. The $12 billion Ford cut would have been a straight 12 percent rebate of 1974 taxes with a $1,000 ceiling. The bulk of the Congressional cut for individuals consisted of (a) an $8 billion rebate of 1974 taxes graduated downward as a percentage of incomes, (b)

an $8 billion continuing reduction in the form of a tax credit and enlarged minimum and standard deductions benefiting especially low and middle income earners, (c) a $1.5 billion earned income credit for low-income workers, and (d) a $1.7 billion special payment to the aged and disabled.

- *Speedy payout:* The Ford program had proposed two $6 billion rebate payments in May and September of 1975. As already noted, the Act put $12 billion in taxpayers' hands in April, May, and June.

- *Sustained stimulus:* Unlike the Ford program, which had only the rebate of 1974 taxes for individuals, the Tax Reduction Act provided nearly $12 billion of continued tax cuts for individuals at annual rates in the second half of 1975 and, assuming extension of the cuts, in 1976.

As the tax bonanza started flowing to the public, it was not yet apparent that an end to the recession was at hand—at least an end in the economist's sense that after 18 months, real GNP stopped receding. But an upturn was indeed in the making. The big tax cut, coupled with a dramatic inventory turnaround, was expected to generate a brisk rebound in the economy. Yet, if the economic policy makers—still caught in their inflation psychosis—turned the monetary and fiscal valves down or off too soon, economic expansion might be aborted far short of acceptable employment and output goals. Those were "The Dangers of an Upturn" examined in the following article.

The Dangers of an Upturn

THE WALL STREET JOURNAL *May 13, 1975*

That much heralded business upturn, not far off, will be the economic nonevent of 1975. For while *business* will turn up, unemployment will hang high and unused capacity will be huge. The great danger is that Messrs. Burns and Simon, gaining aid and comfort from the upward *di-*

rection of activity, will ignore the abysmal *level* of the economy and press their Holy War against inflation with recovery-aborting fervor.

Right now, we are in the darkness that comes just before the dawn. Unemployment is still rising, to a peak between 9 and 10 percent. Much consumer demand is being met from inventories instead of new production. Prospects for autos and housing range from feeble to anemic. Plant and equipment outlays are still being marked down.

But as the 1975 tax cuts pour into the economy, as inventories are drawn down and production steps up to meet the consumer, and as the pace of government spending (especially on defense) picks up, the economy should begin a rebound. It should carry real GNP upward at a 6 to 7 percent pace in the second half of the year.

Still and all, the dawn will break cold and gray for the unemployed. The jobless rate will hover near 9 percent throughout 1975. (For an illustrative breakdown of average unemployment by various groups, see Chart 7.) And this year's rebound will not become next year's recovery unless the forces that are turning the economy around are buttressed by monetary and fiscal policies for sustained expansion.

Before tossing our hats in the air at the first signs of an upswing, we should reflect a moment on the time path of the stimulants that will bring it about:

- *Tax cuts:* After pumping money into the economy this quarter at a $50 billion annual rate, the injections will drop to a $15 billion rate in succeeding quarters. (In contrast, the 1964 tax cut, in today's terms, would have produced a sustained $26 billion rate of injection.)
- *Budget stimulus:* Even assuming expenditures in the neighborhood of $365 billion in fiscal 1976 and continuation of about $12 billion of the tax cuts next year, the budget will swing significantly toward restriction (by some $10 to $15 billion in full-employment terms between the first half of 1975 and the first half of 1976) at a time when recovery is still in its early stages.

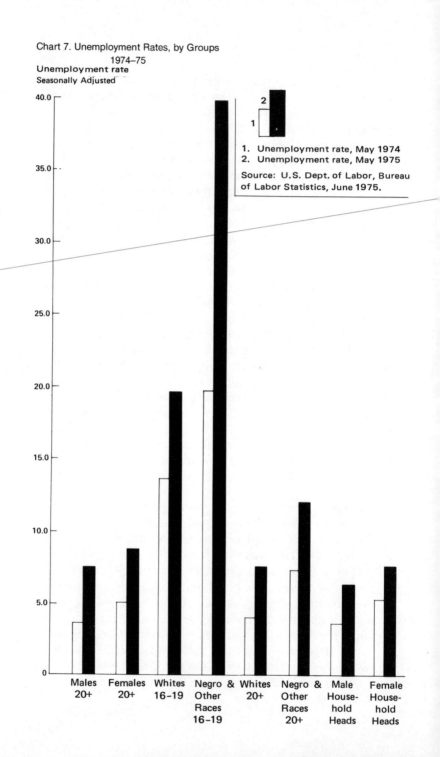

Chart 7. Unemployment Rates, by Groups
1974–75

Unemployment rate
Seasonally Adjusted

1. Unemployment rate, May 1974
2. Unemployment rate, May 1975

Source: U.S. Dept. of Labor, Bureau of Labor Statistics, June 1975.

- *Money supply:* After the temporary current spurt in money supply growth, the Federal Reserve will be tempted to go back to its "standard" 6 percent growth target. If it does, this alone could condemn us to a paltry 4–5 percent rate of increase in real GNP in 1976.
- *Inventories:* The big spur to production implicit in the drop in inventory liquidation rates from a peak of perhaps $20 billion to the neighborhood of zero by the end of the year is hardly likely to be sustained via inventory accumulation in 1976.

Yet under the whiplash of the Ford-Simon-Burns rhetoric, even the *prospect* of an upturn is being used to mobilize the nation's continuing fears of inflation in a campaign against more expansionary budgetary and monetary policy. The upturn itself will give aid and comfort to that campaign. The forces then arrayed against vigorous policies for expansion would indeed be formidable:

- The Federal Reserve, still smarting from charges of election-year overexpansion in 1972, will let its deep-seated anti-inflationary bias be its guide.
- The White House, following its inherent economic conservatism, seems ready to settle for a mild expansion and slow absorption of the unemployed.
- Congress, intimidated by scare-talk about deficits and inflation and determined to demonstrate its fiscal responsibility under the new budget procedures, is likely to be imprudently "prudent." That is, in guarding against the distant threat of renewed inflation, it seems unwilling to deal boldly with today's deep recession.

This dangerously timid and restrictive mood—which, if it persists, could lead us from the 1974–75 recession, after a brief spurt, into a 1976 stagnation—seems to be rooted in neglect of some factors and misperception of others.

First, in its blind preoccupation with inflation, the Fed seems to forget that (a) the ferocious inflation of 1973–74 is rapidly ebbing, (b) there is no reason to expect the forces that generated over one-half of that inflationary up-surge—two years of disastrous crop failures, a quintupling of oil prices, and dollar devaluation—to recur during the expansion of the mid-1970's, and (c) a miserly monetary policy and restrictive fiscal policy would blunt both the up-swing in productivity that can help us subdue inflation in the short run and the expansion of savings and capital spending that can forestall shortages in the longer run.

Second, in assessing the economy's capacity to absorb stimulus, we seem to forget that (a) this recession is twice as deep as any previous postwar recession, (b) while real GNP has dropped 7 percent in the past 18 months, poten-tial GNP has also been rising (by 6 percent, if we use trend growth), thereby idling about $200 billion of our annual productive capacity, and (c) American industry is now operating at only two-thirds of capacity. It remains a chill-ing reality that three consecutive years of 7 percent real growth would still leave unemployment at more than 6 percent and that present policies provide no assurance that even 7 percent growth will be maintained in 1976.

Third, even the redoubtable John Dunlop, in expressing the fear that bottlenecks in primary processing industries will abort recovery, seems to forget (a) that operating rates in primary processing industries are running below 70 per-cent, and (b) that many of the 1973–74 shortages reflected a frenzied flight into commodities—partly protective, partly speculative—as much as, perhaps more than, a genuine scarcity of materials for productive use, and (c) that many of these materials are only now being disgorged in 1975's massive inventory liquidation. True, that inventory liquida-tion makes the huge idle capacity today somewhat decep-tive. But inventory gorging and hoarding also blew the bot-tleneck problem in 1973–74 out of all proportion.

Fourth, two major misapprehensions about the budget continue to plague the country and inhibit the Congress. One myth is that the huge federal budget is somehow the result of government profligacy. The facts are that (a) nearly $60 billion of the projected 1976 deficit is due simply to the ravages of recession (about $45 billion of reduced revenues and $15 billion of increased unemployment costs) and (b) the $4 billion overestimate of offshore oil lease revenues and a $6 billion or so underestimate of domestic expenditures bring Mr. Ford's deficit to some $70 billion—small wonder that Republican Senator Bellmon angrily accuses the White House of "phony" budget numbers.

A companion myth is that civilian spending is the main source of upthrust in the federal budget today. But it is defense purchases, already running several billion dollars above projections, that are programed (according to the Special Analyses section of Mr. Ford's budget) to rise some $25 billion, at annual rates, in the next five quarters. Leaving aside the energy program and the rise in unemployment benefits, the Ford budget for fiscal 1976 projects an 11 percent increase in defense expenditures, 9 percent for income security, 6 percent for health, and zero for education, manpower, and social services.

Fifth, those who shrink from vigorous expansionary policies are also forgetting the huge costs of continued stagnation, not only in the human terms of intolerably high unemployment and intolerable losses of output, but in terms, already mentioned, of the productivity advances and capital formation foregone in a stagnating economy.

Is this an argument for pulling out all the stops? No, but it is an argument for stopping all the pulls—the downward pulls of niggardly monetary policy, a fading tax cut, and parsimonious budget policy.

The Fed should lose no time in assuring the country that it will accommodate expansion, even if this means going beyond the newly declared 5 to 7½ percent monetary growth range.

The Congress should move promptly to make crystal clear, preferably by early reenactment, that the $12 to $13 billion of tax cuts beyond the rebate, social security payments, and housing credit *will* continue in 1976.

Congressional spending and deficit targets should be adjusted to allow an added $5 to $10 billion for recovery programs targeted to areas of high unemployment and effective only as long as national unemployment exceeds a triggering level, e.g., expanded unemployment compensation and public service jobs and a new program of countercyclical assistance to hard-hit state and local governments, all of which would gradually self-destruct as the economy regains its health.

A year from now will be plenty of time for another look at expansionary policies. Even if we follow a resolute program of expansion, one that would boost real GNP at an 8 percent annual rate, we would still find the U.S. economy in mid-1976 with 7½–8 percent unemployment, with output running some $125 billion below its potential, and with shortages and bottlenecks still no threat. That will give us plenty of time to review the bidding and determine whether, when, and how restraint should be applied. To do it at the first sign of an economic upturn would be an abject confession of economic bankruptcy.

The danger of an upturn, then, is that the Burns-Simon axis will mistake the warm and gentle zephyrs of the rebound for the gathering winds of a new inflation—to be leaned against in the best (or worst) Fed tradition and to be used as a club against bold Congressional action. The consequence? The rebound may never become a recovery. If the White House and the Fed, hypnotized by the fear of inflation, quickly turn from expansion to restriction, they will snatch defeat from the jaws of victory.

In the summer of 1975, it appeared that the policy dangers foreseen in the previous article might be materializing:

- The Federal Reserve—reacting to the vigor of the economic rebound, to a June spurt in food and fuel prices, and even more to the big jump in money supply as tax cuts temporarily flowed into demand deposits—began to tighten money and boost short-term interest rates in July.

- The Congress—responding to the new budget ceiling provisions of the Congressional Budget Control and Impoundment Act of 1974, even though they did not become mandatory until 1976—seemed determined to hold to the $69 billion deficit and $367 billion expenditure ceiling it had set in May 1975.
- The White House—apprehensive about the size of the deficit and the new upturn in the Consumer Price Index in early summer—gave every indication of backtracking on fiscal stimulus as the year wore on.

Recognizing these threats that might turn a robust rebound into an anemic expansion, Speaker Carl Albert convened the House Steering and Policy Committee for an unprecedented hearing on economic policy. My opening statement to that Committee on July 24 tried to find common ground on which Congress, the White House, and the Federal Reserve might join in promoting and prolonging expansion without unleashing a new inflation. Excerpts from that statement are presented below.

A Liberal-Conservative Program for Expansion

STATEMENT BEFORE THE HOUSE
STEERING AND POLICY COMMITTEE *July 24, 1975*

Apparently, the combination of an on-schedule turnaround in the economy, the liklihood of a considerable rebound (perhaps at a 7 percent rate of real growth in the next nine months or so), and the prospect of moderating inflation have sent the White House into an orbit of joy.

Nor is this mood likely to be dispelled in the next few months by the indexes of output, GNP, profits, and inflation. As consumers spend their tax rebates and producers restock their shelves, the economy is beginning its long climb out of the depths of our worst postwar recession.

All that will be left behind is human beings—the nine to

ten million unemployed (including part-time and discouraged workers) who won't find jobs on the gentle slopes of recovery.

Indeed, even with a year of steady recovery at, say, a 7 percent clip, unemployment would still hover near 8 percent, that is, above the worst levels reached at the trough of any previous postwar recession. Excess capacity would abound—from today's 66 percent operating rates in manufacturing, we might have moved all the way up to 75 percent—again, still a recessionary level by the test of our five previous recessions since World War II.

Given the long lead times in economic policy, any euphoria about the present should quickly be replaced by concern about the future. In order to convert rebound into recovery, make major inroads on unemployment, and stop the appalling waste of $200 billion a year of our productive capacity, Congress and the White House should be hammering out a 1975 economic action program for sustained recovery without rekindled inflation in 1976.

Instead, we find something close to stalemate. The Congress seems to be cowed by the brandishing of the deficit specter and the veto sword. As a result, it is being tarred with a do-nothing brush. But on the economic front, perhaps the real culprit is a do-nothing White House. It seems inclined to do nothing more to strengthen the forces of recovery; to do nothing to keep the grip of the tax system and the budget from tightening once again in 1976; to do nothing to assure the unemployed, the consumer, and business that expansion will be the order of the day until the American economy again nears the limits of its huge productive potential.

Can Congress, the White House, and the Federal Reserve System find common ground on which to provide that assurance? I don't see why not.

The centerpiece of the program must be an assured continuation of tax relief into 1976. And cheek-by-jowl with a move to avoid the untimely death of the 1975 tax cuts should be further tax reductions (a) to keep the Federal fiscal noose from tightening again in the face of intolerable unemployment and slack in the economy and (b) to keep oil price increases from eroding purchasing power and undermining economic recovery.

A sizable net tax cut for 1976 would clearly be good liberal medicine, an effective antidote for the massive unemployment that plagues the economy. And it would also accord with the best of conservative doctrine:

- In an economy subject to endemic inflation, nominal or money income—on which taxes are based—rises faster than real income. Add the element of progression, and the result is that Federal taxes rise steadily and stealthily as a proportion of real income and GNP—surely not a consummation devoutly to be wished by conservatives.
- Congress could remove this fiscal overburden by expanding government programs. Or it could index the income tax, thereby adjusting it continually for inflation. But that would provide tax relief in both recession and boom.
- The coupling of liberal and conservative objectives could be realized by periodic tax cuts (a) so designed as to remove the tax overburden fastened on us by inflation and (b) so timed as to boost a lagging economy.
- In short, the tax cut for 1976 could serve the interests of longer-run fiscal neutrality (in an aggregative sense) while providing vital short-run stimulus needed for sustained recovery.

On the expenditure side, guidelines for an antirecession or prorecovery policy seem reasonably clear:

- Don't increase *baseline* expenditures to fight recessions or promote recovery, that is, for anticyclical reasons alone.
- But do provide generously for public service jobs, antirecession grants to hard-hit cities and states, and perhaps—in this deep and stubborn a recession—some public works speed-ups. Trigger them to come on

stream only at high unemployment levels and to self-destruct when unemployment drops below, say, 5½ percent.

- Such programs move people from relief rolls to payrolls, serve to get badly needed jobs done, and phase out as the private economy returns to prosperity. Once again, the liberal and conservative objectives coalesce.

Next, what about the interplay of Congressional budget policy and Federal Reserve monetary policy? Let me urge you not to forget the trade-offs here. If the Fed jumps to the ramparts of tighter money every time it hears a twig crack—as it did in late June, with predictable shell-shock in the money and capital markets—the Congress will have to raise its sights on budgetary stimulus accordingly.

But if you could strike a bargain with the Fed to pursue a "hold harmless" policy of essentially stable interest rates in the early stages of recovery in exchange for greater fiscal restraint, your antirecession tax cuts and budget programs could be correspondingly smaller. The net result would be an agreed policy for economic expansion tilted toward investment stimulus, not via tax-incentive gimmicks, but instead by promoting lower interest rates and shifting some funds from consumption into savings.

Won't a program of tax cuts and temporary expenditure programs risk a rekindling of inflation and an overdose of deficits? No.

Neither excess demand nor a new round of commodity inflation (oil price jumps and crop failures aside) is anywhere in sight:

- Even two or three years of economic expansion at a 7–8 percent real growth rate won't press against the economy's supply potential.
- As for commodity inflation, it's true that the June jump in food and gasoline prices is a sobering reminder of where inflation forecasts went wrong in 1973–74. But with economic recovery lagging in the rest of the indus-

trialized world, with rosy U.S. crop prospects, and with the dollar strengthening, only oil looms as a threat here.

- The greater threat may well be the concentrated industries and powerful labor unions that appear to be more and more impervious to competitive forces and to the effects of massive unemployment and excess capacity. The Council on Wage and Price Stability may find—indeed, I believe *will* find—that it needs considerably more than subpoena power to cope with this threat.

Finally, what about the deficit constraint under the new congressional budget procedure? Can a $69 billion deficit limit accommodate an adequate fiscal policy for sustained recovery?

- A $69-billion-deficit budget is a next-to-no stimulus budget. It cushions but does not propel.
- The recession alone accounts for a shortfall of about $50 billion in federal revenues and a boost of nearly $20 billion in unemployment and related benefits.
- To do the fiscal policy job needed to insure vigorous recovery plainly demands an expansion of the $69 billion ceiling.

So far, all the risks have been centered on a too-slow recovery, too-high unemployment, and too-big sacrifice of output. It's time for Congress to redress the balance of risks.

As the country began to breathe a bit easier about both recession and inflation, other economic problems began to compete for the policy maker's attention. One of the most hotly debated topics in the second half of 1975 was the so-called "capital shortfall." Not that it was an immediate or pressing problem in either the real or financial sense. Surely, with factories operating at less than 70 percent of capacity and output running about $175 billion below existing productive potential, plenty of real capital resources were available. And after private demands on money and capital markets had shrunk by some $70 to $80 billion during the recession, there was no shortage in the sense of financial strains that might curb capital formation.

But the memories of shortages and financial stress were still fresh in people's minds. Bottlenecks in the primary processing industries like steel, copper, paper, aluminum, and chemicals had appeared sooner than expected in the 1972–73 boom. And the energy crisis required huge investments in oil, coal, nuclear, and even more exotic types of energy. Antipollution and safety outlays in response to government requirements were averaging up to perhaps 10 percent of business spending for plant and equipment.

On the financial side, the economy had just gone through a trying period, dubbed by some a "liquidity crisis." Businesses had had to resort increasingly to outside sources of funds, mostly bank loans, commercial paper, and bonds—with equity capital, new stock issues, playing only a minor role. During the 1950's and early 1960's, internal cash flows—retained profits and capital consumption allowances—provided three-quarters of the funds needed for plant and equipment spending and inventory and other working capital needs. But by 1974, the ratio had dropped to one-half. In this process, U.S. business shifted from a position of borrowing only 60 cents for each one dollar of its internal cash flow in 1964 to borrowing one dollar and 60 cents for each dollar by 1974. And the ratio of short-term to long-term debt grew sharply, while the ratio of liquid assets to short-term debt dropped to a new postwar low in 1974.

The liquidity squeeze was no optical illusion. But by 1975, it was rapidly relaxing its grip. As so often happens with economic phenomena, perception lagged behind reality:

- Reliance on outside sources to finance business investment dropped from 49 percent in 1974 to 22 percent in the first nine months of 1975.
- After hitting a postwar low as a proportion of cor-

porate gross receipts in 1974, profits streaked upward in 1975.

- Corporations scrambled to restore their liquidity by converting inventory into cash, repaying debt, and the like.

In other words, profits and liquidity were making a remarkable comeback. But both data delays and, more importantly, highly visible financial troubles— several bank failures, bankruptcy of the chain-store giant W. T. Grant, the parlous condition of many real estate investment trusts, New York City's woes—obscured the underlying improvement. Beneath the turbulent surface, the financial waters were beginning to run much quieter and deeper.

This is not to suggest that an earlier recognition of improving financial health would have blunted the Ford Administration's drive to do something about the "capital shortage." And "doing something" meant providing tax incentives for—or more euphemistically, removing tax impediments to—business incentives to invest. Republican administrations had no patent on this approach—in its first major tax reduction, the Kennedy Administration in 1962 had liberalized depreciation guidelines and introduced the 7 percent investment tax credit.

But the Ford-Simon program—which caught the Congress both unawares and uninterested—took a deeper cut at the problem. Late in July 1975, Secretary Simon proposed a "tax program for increased national saving" to take effect in 1977. It consisted of roughly $1 billion of special tax breaks for individual savings and a combination of dividend deductions and stockholder credits to reduce the "double taxation" of corporate income at an eventual cost of about $13 billion a year. The proposals were accompanied by a barrage of arguments for more capital formation and for removing the "tax bias against saving."

The following article addresses itself to the general concept of the capital shortage and to the Treasury proposals for stepping up the rate of private savings and investment.

Taxes and the "Capital Shortfall"

THE WALL STREET JOURNAL *August 19, 1975*

"Taxation, like love, is not wholly founded on reason," Justice Frankfurter once said. Nothing illustrates that truism better than the Ford-Simon proposal for new tax spurs for investment. They demonstrate all too well how hard it is to resolve an economic policy issue on facts and analysis alone. They bristle with value choices. For example:

- How much economic growth does the country "need" or want, and how much consumption are we willing to forgo to get it?
- How much of the nation's capital investment should flow into the human brainpower and skills, how much into public infrastructure, and how much into plant and equipment?
- Are new tax incentives for business capital spending worth the cost in tax equity, in new tax benefits for the well-to-do and new inequalities in tax burdens of persons with equal income?

No amount of economic logic can resolve these issues. To arrive at policy recommendations, the economist—like others—has to carry his ideological baggage with him. But en route, he can help sort out fiction from fact and rhetoric from reality, he can define and clarify the issues, and he can estimate the probable costs and benefits of alternative solutions. Narrowing the gap between rhetoric and reality is an important first step toward a balanced judgment in the "capital shortage" controversy.

Rhetoric: U.S. private investment is in a disturbing downtrend.

Reality: The ratio of business fixed investment to GNP (in constant prices), after hovering right around 10 percent from 1946 to 1964, posted a gain to 11 percent in the

1965–74 decade, including an uptick to 11.3 percent in 1973–74.

Rhetoric: While not on our doorstep today, the capital shortage lies just across the threshold of economic recovery.

Reality: With operating rates in manufacturing running at postwar lows—below 70 percent both overall and in "major materials industries,"—a Citibank study concludes that even with 7 percent to 8 percent in real GNP in 1976–77, "there would be ample manpower as well as physical capacity" as we entered 1978. A Data Resources study agrees and adds, "On present prospects, even the later 1970's should not see major bottlenecks."

Rhetoric: But, say true believers like Secretary Simon, add up the "capital requirements" of the U.S. economy between 1975 and 1985—for energy, transportation, primary processing industries and all the rest—and you arrive at a scary (and implicitly unmanageable) total of $4.5 trillion.

Reality: Breaking this staggering total into annual increments and relating it to rising GNP and savings flows not only makes it easier to grasp but brings it within reach. A half-dozen independent studies of capital adequacy—the Bosworth-Duesenberry-Carron study for Brookings is the most comprehensive—take this approach and arrive at persuasively similar conclusions:

- Overall investment needs will average roughly 16 percent of GNP. Business demand for capital will account for about 11 percent of this total. Both numbers are roughly one percentage point above the postwar averages.
- Private savings will fall about one percentage point short of meeting the projected needs.
- To close the gap will require public savings in the form of a federal budget surplus equal to the private savings shortfall (plus any state-local deficits). The Brookings study foresees the need for a high employment surplus of $15 billion to $20 billion by 1980.

Those who would regard a federal surplus as pie in the sky should bear in mind (a) that remarkable changes in congressional budget procedures and mood are taking place and (b) that, given the projected growth of about $200 billion in high-employment tax revenues by 1980, achieving the target surplus requires only that budget increases and tax cuts in the next five years be held to $180 billion, or so.

Rhetoric: Unless we redouble our efforts to stimulate capital formation, other industrial countries will outstrip us. Their tax systems are kinder to business and capital than ours, hence investment burgeons, growth flowers and the U.S. is left far behind.

Reality: That's almost as slippery a syllogism as "Some dogs have fleas; my dog has fleas; ergo, my dog is *some* dog." Not that our growth rate has kept up with theirs. Even adjusting for two Nixon-Fed recessions, the percentage growth in productivity and GNP in Germany, France, Italy, Canada and Japan ranged from moderately to sharply above ours in the past decade.

But the chain of reasoning ignores the large role of catch-ups in technology, in mass education, in transfers of labor out of agriculture into industry as major factors in the other countries' more robust growth rate. And it glosses over the fact that those economies have a long way to go, that "catch-up" is not the same as "overtake." A recent Treasury study shows U.S. productivity still tops in the world. Output per employed civilian in Japan and Italy has moved up to about two-thirds, and in France and Germany to four-fifths of the United States.

As growth authority Edward Denison has put it, "Nothing in [my] analysis suggests that the conditions making for higher European growth would continue to operate if the European countries were to reach American levels of national income per person employed."

Rhetoric: Refuse to spur capital formation by tax relief and you will kill the goose that lays the golden eggs.

Reality: Several geese lay the golden eggs of growth. To

cite just one example, Denison's studies show that from 1948 to 1969, roughly half of the rise in output per worker and one-third of the rise in total output came from advances in knowledge.

Rhetoric: The U.S. tax system hits business and the wealthy too hard and thus chokes off risk capital supplies and incentives.

Reality: While "too hard" is all too subjective, some objective facts suggest that the tax blow may be softer (or less debilitating) than supposed:

- Studies by Joseph Pechman show that the effective tax rate on corporate net income is closer to 35 percent than the statutory rate of 48 percent and that, as a proportion of gross profits, corporate taxes were reduced from 37 percent in 1953 to 27 percent in 1972.
- The investment credit alone will save corporate and individual investors some $9 billion this fiscal year.
- Generous tax shelters and tax cuts—the top marginal rate, 91 percent a dozen years ago, has been cut to 50 percent on earned income and 70 percent on investment income—have held the effective rate of the federal individual income tax to 30 percent of economic income for persons with incomes about $100,000.
- In the good old days of low taxes and little progressivity, circa 1929, the nation's savings and investments came to 16 percent of GNP. In the bad new days of high and progressive taxes, circa 1973, the ratio happened to be the same 16 percent.

Stripping the capital shortage issue of rhetorical overkill and specious assertions is not tantamount to destroying the case for higher levels of business capital formation or tax spurs to achieve them. As one of the midwives at the birth of the investment credit (and the liberalizing of depreciation guidelines) in 1962 and as an advocate of an enlarged investment credit in 1974, I have on occasion pressed the case myself. I regard it as an open question whether private savings flows will be adequate to meet the country's future growth aspirations. And I share the deep concern over excessive reliance on debt financing of business investment.

But that is a far cry from concluding that the solution lies in untaxing dividends, savings, and business income. The Ford-Simon proposal to stimulate investment by a $13 billion-a-year tax cut for corporations and investors is a case in point. As a one-dimensional program in a multidimensional world, it simply won't pass muster. It lacks not just political grace, but economic balance and a reasoned sense of priorities.

In today's economy, beset not by a capital shortage but by a severe job shortage and low sales volume, it would have been the better part of both wisdom and grace to call first—or at least simultaneously—for action to expand jobs and markets by continuing the 1975 tax cut into 1976. (Indeed, if the tax cut expires at year-end, consumer buying power will be hit by a $12 billion downdraft as tax withholding rates jump.) And, as a bonus, Mr. Simon would hit pay dirt on the capital formation front far faster than through changes in tax structure. Nearly $20 billion a year of savings and investment is being lost as a hostage to recession.

For the longer pull, one would have expected some concern over the impact of a $13 billion annual tax loss (plus unspecified tax cuts to boost individuals' savings) on the federal deficit and the consequent undermining of the Treasury's ability to help make ends meet in the capital markets. By his own lights, Mr. Simon should be aiming at an eventual full employment surplus to facilitate an easier money policy and nourish the capital markets. Tax breaks for business would seem to rank a good deal lower than the appropriate fiscal-monetary mix as nutrients for economic growth.

The Ford-Simon approach is also rendered suspect—indeed, is weakened both economically and politically—by its myopic focus on tax cuts for business and investors as the chosen path to greater capital formation.

It would surely carry more conviction if its concept of

tax reform embraced an attack on the costly tax preferences that warp the allocation of capital and other resources, for example, real estate tax shelters, capital gains
treatment for timber and cattle, the $1.3 billion annual tax
bonus to DISCs, and the exclusion of capital gains at
death, costing $5 billion a year. Or is one to assume that
the Administration approves of any and all tax favors for
any and all forms of investment, no matter what they cost
in terms of efficiency and equity?

Perhaps that same line of reasoning ruled out any
thought of balancing the tax treatment of dividends and
interest not by untaxing dividends but by taxing interest.
That is, following Henry Wallich's suggestion, disallow interest (on future debt, at least) as a deduction from taxable
income, and plow the proceeds into reductions in the 48
percent corporate tax rate.

Little need be said about the obvious inroads on the progressivity of the tax system that are part and parcel of the
Ford-Simon approach. Had their package included some
cutbacks in unwarranted tax shelters for business and the
wealthy together with a call for a continuance of the 1975
tax breaks for modest incomes (liberalized minimum and
standard deductions and tax credits), it would have shown
some responsiveness to public and congressional concepts
of fairness in taxation. Ignoring these assured the program
of the chilly reception it deserved.

The Congress simply ignored the Ford-Simon tax proposal. And even the President's own Budget and Economic Messages in January 1976 gave it short shrift.
The budget mentioned only in passing that "integra-
tion of individual and corporation income taxation as outlined in Administration testimony last July is
also proposed effective January 1, 1978."

The 1976 *Economic Report* apparently omitted it entirely. Indeed, in Chapter 1, the Council of Economic
Advisers reported the results of a special study of capital
requirements and came up with only the mild suggestion that "increased savings incentives may have to sup-
plement increased investment incentives. . . ." Even

this would depend not only on business investment needs "but also on the demands for residential construction and net foreign investment." The Council added that beyond 1980, "there may be no need to maintain higher business fixed investment to GNP ratios than in previous periods of high employment. . . ."

The Pace of Recovery

In spite of the snappy pace of the economic rebound—real GNP growth, starting in the April-June quarter at a 3.3 percent annual rate, spurted to a 12 percent pace in the summer quarter thanks to the tax hypodermic and the huge inventory swing (before subsiding to a more sedate 5 percent pace in the fourth quarter)—there were many clouds on the policy horizon in early fall:

- Extension of the 1975 tax cut, soon to be voted by Congress, might be vetoed by the President.
- Money was still tightening, and short-term interest rates were rising.
- There was no assurance that the energy bill, working its way slowly through Congress midst cliff-hanging postponements of the expiration of all oil price controls, would be signed by the President. Failure to enact it would mean an abrupt jump in oil prices (by some $10 billion), thus giving a jolt to inflation and putting another crimp in consumer purchasing power.
- Another Hairbreadth-Harry drama was playing in New York, as the country's foremost city teetered on the brink of bankruptcy—with consequent queasiness not just in the municipal bond market, but in other securities markets as well.

In mid-October, George Perry and I addressed ourselves to the fiscal, monetary, and energy uncertainties as part of our forecast that the economy would grow at a brisk 7 percent pace in 1976:

- "On *tax cuts*, our best guess is that Congress will follow through on its intention to protect consumers from a jump in the income tax withholding rate next January 1 by extending the tax cut at a $12 billion annual rate. Even if this action is not accompanied by the spending cut called for under Mr. Ford's new cut-and-slash formula, we assume that the extension will become law. [In October, the President recommended a $28 billion cut in taxes (consisting of about $17 billion in renewal of the 1975 cuts and $11 billion of new cuts) to take effect January 1, 1976 and a matching cut of $28 billion in projected fiscal 1977 spending, effective October 1, 1977. The Congress ignored the recommendation—but the President reiterated it in his January 1977 Budget Message.]
- "On *spending*, we expect the Congress—hewing to its tough new budget procedures and spurred by the public's antispending mood—to be restrained in its budgetary actions.
- "On *monetary policy* . . . given the vast slack in the economy, the slow money growth since June, and the emergence of a tighter budget policy than might have been expected, the leeway for a more accommodative monetary policy is clearly present. And the pressures to move toward such a policy in the period ahead are likely to be strong. We are not suggesting that the Fed will succumb to the heat of the 1976 presidential campaign. But we are suggesting that the monetary authorities will not want to take responsibility for . . . a petering out of the U.S. recovery.
- "On *oil prices*, we assume that the battle between the White House and Congress will be resolved without abrupt decontrol of old oil prices, that is, without inflicting a large new "tax" on consumers and thus retarding recovery. Gradual decontrol seems more likely."

Policy unfolded according to this script. Before the year was out, Ford overrode strong opposition in his Administration, especially from Treasury Secretary Simon, to sign the energy bill authorizing phased decontrol of oil prices over 40 months (and mandating more fuel-efficient cars, stockpiling of crude oil, and so forth). At the eleventh hour, he signed the bill extending the tax cut after it was amended to include some face-saving but in no sense binding language about budget cuts. And the Federal Reserve did indeed relent with the result that the summer bulge in short-term interest rates was more than erased, and long-term rates fell as well.

New York City and Fiscal Brinksmanship

What of the specter of New York bankruptcy that hung over the economy? The city was drowning in a sea of woes brought on by its own financial mismanagement, by its disproportionate welfare burdens, by the recession-induced erosion of its revenues and ballooning welfare costs, and by the "core-city disease" in virulent form. Each calls for comment:

- *Financial mismanagement:* For years, the city had been borrowing money and piling up debt to meet current expenses, had succumbed to union pressures for high wages and sky-high pensions, and deluded itself and others about the state of its finances.
- *Welfare burdens:* New York had borne larger burdens than any other American city through the huge influx of immigrants from abroad and later from the South and Puerto Rico. According to city officials, New York City bears an annual burden of some $800 million for welfare and related costs that other large U.S. cities do not have to bear.
- *Recession:* New York has consistently had higher unemployment rates than the country as a whole; indeed,

in the fall of 1975 New York found its unemployment rates rising to 12 percent while the national rate was falling toward 8 percent.

• *The core-city problem:* As the high-cost population moves in and becomes mired in the core city, the well-to-do and business activity move out, thus depleting the tax base and requiring higher tax rates in a vicious spiral. And when New York City was forced to push up its tax rates, Connecticut and, until 1976, New Jersey beckoned with the lure of freedom from state income taxes.

As the New York financial situation grew shakier in 1975, the city found it could no longer go to the private capital markets for funds. Even with the aid of a special Municipal Assistance Corporation (to which it ceded important fiscal powers), the city again was given the cold shoulder after some initial borrowing. Its plight was desperate.

Where lay the national responsibility? Late in October, President Ford gave his answer. Sternly lecturing New York on its fiscal sins and stonily rejecting its pleas for a federal "bail-out," he said there was none, except to help the city maintain services after going bankrupt. Again and again the theme was sounded, especially by Secretary Simon, that New York had made its bed and could lie in it and that allowing New York to go bankrupt would have no dire "ripple" effects on the financial markets, indeed, might clear the air. But the jittery responses of the bond and stock markets to every twist and turn of the New York crisis seemed to belie this assurance.

To a growing number of observers (judging by the public opinion polls), it appeared that there was indeed a national responsibility (a) to avoid the potentially serious repercussions on municipal financing generally and (b) to give some type of special assistance to a city that was burdened with far more than its share of the nation's economically lame, halt, and blind.

Meanwhile, the stock market rose when it looked as though New York might make it, only to fall again when the winds blew the other way. The only thing that rose steadily was the national mood of anxiety. The spectacle of one hasty improvisation after another, of continued dissembling by the New York financial authorities, and the game of "chicken" played by the White House (if that's what it was) was hardly an edifying one.

But, as it so often does, the American democratic process muddled through once more to a fairly sensible interim solution: Reversing himself completely (some said "simply playing out his cleverly conceived poker hand"), the President on November 26 proposed—and the Congress quickly approved—strictly tiding-over assistance to New York in the form of $2.3 billion of temporary loans to New York City to be repaid within the year as revenues flowed in.

In spite of an audible nationwide sigh of relief, the New York problem was by no means solved. Bankruptcy was averted, but the basic problem remained for New York and for other rotting-core cities. Even with large doses of self-discipline, financial reform, and belt-tightening (and it was not clear that New York was doing enough on these fronts), the grinding problems of welfare costs, recession impacts, and the core-city syndrome remained as threats to solvency.

As the various policy roadblocks to expansion were removed, at least temporarily, the central policy emphasis gradually returned to basics. How much leeway did the U.S. economy have for expansionary stimulus without inflationary consequences? In any rational policy-making process, that question had to be answered before deciding how large a second-stage offensive against unemployment and economic slack it would be prudent to mount. The following article, "How Much Headroom for Expansion?" was one attempt to formulate that answer.

How Much Headroom For Expansion?

THE WALL STREET JOURNAL *December 18, 1975*

Strange as it seems, U.S. economic policy is already ducking its head for fear of eventually running into capacity ceilings. How else can one explain the consuming fear of demand-pull inflation that, the current respite aside, stays the hand of the Federal Reserve? Or that leads Secretary Simon to the dark foreboding that failure to match the tax cut extension with budget cuts is fraught with inflationary danger (though, asymmetrically, other Ford advisers assure us that failure to extend the tax cut would not be a big enough thing to impede economic recovery).

Not that the issue of capacity or GNP potential—the output and employment limits beyond which the U.S. economy overheats—is a minor or insignificant one in plotting the path of prudent policy. Looking two, three, or four years down the road, we have to recognize and respect these limits as a vital policy determinant. Indeed, an appraisal of these limits is the point of this exercise.

But to avoid any misunderstanding about immediate policy: As we just begin to emerge from the economy's deepest plunge in nearly 40 years—and at a time when unemployment (in terms of labor time lost) is still over 9 percent, when industrial operating rates are just above 70 percent of capacity, and when even conservative estimates of unused potential see well over $100 billion of economic slack, of productive capacity running to waste, each year— it seems almost bizarre that the President is poised to veto a tax cut extension and thereby activate a tax increase.

Even worse, if a tax cut veto were to be flanked by a veto of the oil bill—and both vetoes were sustained—the White House could be ushering in the New Year with abrupt jumps in both taxes and oil prices. If, to complete this bleak picture, the Federal Reserve quickly returns to its Spartan monetary posture, the three major forces that dragged us into the deep recession of 1974–75 would be reactivated as a drag on recovery in 1976.

That this "worst case" will materialize is not likely. But what many of us would regard as the "best case"—a considerably more expansionary monetary policy plus measures to avert a tightening of fiscal policy in 1976–77—is also less than likely. Indeed, it seems to be quite outside the bounds of White House, Federal Reserve, and even most Congressional thinking today.

No one denies that a 6 percent rate of inflation calls for prudence and moderation in policies for recovery. But if the U.S. economy is in fact moving at a pace well below the speed limits of expansion and won't reach its capacity limits for several years, present policies have to be rated as imprudent and immoderate—as trading far too much in lost jobs, output, income, and tax revenues for far too little gain on the inflation front.

That calls for a brief look at the speed of recovery and a more searching look at the U.S. economic potential. The recovery, after a tax-assisted takeoff last summer, seems to be settling in at a more sedate pace:

- From a 12 percent rate of advance in real GNP in the third quarter, the pace seems to have dropped to perhaps 5 percent in the current quarter.

- Economic forecasts for 1976 cluster around a 5½ percent to 6 percent real GNP increase—those of us who see something closer to 7 percent are viewed as unrealistic optimists.

- For perspective, put the 1975–76 recovery in the context of the five previous postwar cycles: From a starting point last April far below the trough of any of those cycles—in terms of rates of unemployment, unused capacity, and the like—the current recovery will by the end of 1976 carry us only to the average trough levels of the five previous recessions.

In this picture, we find little cause for exuberance or even satisfaction with the pace of recovery and little support for pussyfooting expansionary policies.

Any misgivings, then, about a bolder approach must relate to the limitations of our economic potential, in either global or bottleneck terms. Does a reasonable appraisal of today's U.S. economic potential, of predicted labor force composition and growth, of productivity trends, and of capacity developments in particular industries provide a basis for lowering our economic sights and pulling in our policy horns? Without providing definitive answers on each point, one can identify important clues that the policy makers should heed before putting further roadblocks in the path of recovery.

It may be useful to start with some boxcar measures of the overall GNP gap, the shortfall of *actual* from *potential* output.

A seat-of-the-pants approach tells us that if the annual rate of real GNP slid, nearly 8 percent from peak to trough (from November 1973 to April 1975) and if the annual trend growth of U.S. economic potential continued at 4 percent during those 18 months, a gap of nearly 14 percent had opened up by last April.* (See Chart 8.) This calculation takes off not from some hypothetical target rate of unemployment, but from the 4.7 percent rate prevailing at the peak month of the cycle.

Rounding this out conservatively to a 5 percent target rate of unemployment, and allowing for some capacity pressures in late 1973, one finds that the shortfall, or gap, or economic slack in the economy comes out to about 12 percent of potential GNP (just under $1.7 trillion in the second quarter of 1975), or about $200 billion a year.

Critics of this calculation may claim that in the face of the severe recession of 1974–75, the U.S. output potential did not in fact expand by the usual 4 percent a year. But this misses the point that a *trend* growth rate of 4 percent does not mean that potential grows that much *every year*. In a deep and prolonged recession, capital spending slackens and productivity plunges. But on the upswing, as

* Later revisions by the Commerce Department put the real GNP slide from the fourth quarter of 1973 to the first quarter of 1975 at 6.6 percent. The numbers in the text would be only marginally affected.

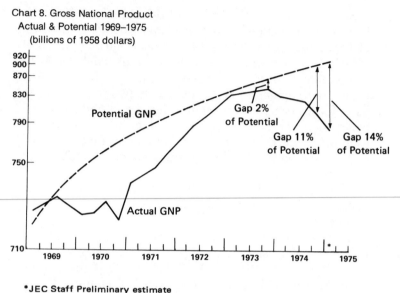

Chart 8. Gross National Product
Actual & Potential 1969–1975
(billions of 1958 dollars)

*JEC Staff Preliminary estimate

Sources: Department of Commerce. Council of Economic Advisers,
Joint Economic Committee

in the present recovery, productivity zooms and capital spending makes up for lost time.

Cross-checking this rough approximatiion of the GNP gap both with Okun's Law and with official projections, one comes up with very similar numbers. Under Okun's Law that each 1 percent change in unemployment translates into a 3 percent change in GNP, the near-9 percent rate of unemployment in the second quarter translates into a 15 percent, or $253 billion, deficiency in GNP at a 4 percent target rate of unemployment and a 12 percent, or $203 billion, deficiency at 5 percent.

The official Commerce Department calculations, based on a 4 percent target unemployment rate and a 4 percent annual growth of GNP potential since 1965, show gaps of $245 billion in the second quarter and $218 billion in the third. Adjusting these to the 5 percent standard brings us once more to the $200 billion, or 12 percent, gap figure at the trough of the recession and to about $172 billion in the third quarter of 1975.

This somewhat tedious exercise is undertaken to show that, no matter how one slices it, there is an ample layer of unused overall capacity in the U.S. economy today—so ample that even the most pusillanimous of policy makers need not be frightened by the specter of excess-demand inflation in 1976—nor in 1977, for that matter.

But that does not settle the issue. Perhaps bottlenecks in critical industries—the primary processing industries, metals in particular—will surprise us and invalidate the global ceilings, as they did in late 1973. Perhaps—but not likely.

Close inspection of the industry-by-industry capital spending performance in 1972–75 is cause for reassurance on this score. Responding to shortages and high prices, the primary processing industries have maintained vigorous capital spending programs even in the face of severe recession, for example:

- In "primary metals" manufacturing, spending for new plant and equipment kept right on rising from an annual rate of $3.6 billion in the second half of 1973 to $6.1 billion in the first half of 1975 and is projected at $6.2 billion in the first half of 1976.
- In the steel industry, outlays on blast furnaces rose from $1.4 billion to $2.9 billion to $3.3 billion in the same time periods.

McGraw-Hill surveys of capacity utilization tell a similarly reassuring story. As a percent of *preferred* operating rates, utilization rates in the primary processing industries dropped from 94 percent at the end of 1973 to 77 percent in mid-1975. In steel, the drop was from 95 percent in December 1973 to 70 percent in September 1975; in nonferrous metals, from 84 to 71½ percent; in paper, from 100 to 78½ percent, and so on.

The data on overall capacity and potential bottlenecks may be reassuring, yet those of little faith in U.S. productive potential still have three other lines of defense.

First, as one careless critic put it, plant and equipment spending in recent years "has gone mostly to satisfy antipollution and safety legislation." The actual Commerce survey figure for pollution abatement for all industries for 1974 was 5.8 percent of total business fixed investment. (Some industries are, of course, impacted much more heavily than others: for all manufacturing, the figure was 10 percent and for primary metals, 23 percent.) Current projections suggest that another 5 or 6 percent will have to be spent to meet safety requirements. A total of 10 to 12 percent for these purposes is not insignificant. But it is a far cry from "mostly."

Second, some observers fear that we are undergoing a serious decline in the trend rate of productivity advance. They seem to be confusing cyclical with secular movements. In a deep and prolonged downturn, everything cyclical begins to look permanent. But closer inspection of the numbers seems to bear out the conclusion of the Data Resources study prepared for the National Commission on Productivity and Work Quality in December 1974 that "there is no evidence to suggest that the overall productivity performance of the American economy has deteriorated":

- Output per man-hour in the private economy, after rising at a 3½ percent rate from 1960 to 1968, dipped briefly during the mild recession of 1969.
- From the first quarter of 1970 to the first quarter of 1973, it rose at a 4 percent annual rate, and then dropped at a 1½ percent annual rate for two years before turning up in the second quarter this year.
- In the third quarter, it rose at a spectacular annual rate of some 11 percent—and under the benign impact of expansion and gap-closing, one can expect above-trend increases in productivity for the 1976–80 period as a whole.

One finds in these numbers no basis for lowering the trend productivity growth of 2.5 percent a year used by the

Council of Economic Advisers (together with a 1.5 percent annual growth in net man hours) in calculating the 4 percent annual growth rate in U.S. economic potential.

Third, some of those who foresee a shrinking growth rate in U.S. potential rest their case in part on a slower growth of the labor force. But again, there is little evidence of this. Annual growth of the labor force from 1970 to 1975 has averaged slightly over 2 percent. With about four million persons, on the average, turning 18 each year between now and 1982, with female labor force participation still expanding, with retirements still running far below (about half) entries, and with entrants of the past decade now moving into the most productive age groups, the prospects are for continued vigorous growth of the U.S. labor pool.

What is the import of all this? While we can't precisely measure the amount of slack in the U.S. economy today, it is crystal clear that there is lots of it. We have plenty of headroom, legroom, hiproom, shoulder-room, and elbow-room for expansion. Nothing in today's projected rates of recovery or policy thinking in Washington suggests a pace of expansion that will test the limits of our capacity or arouse the devil of excess-demand inflation in 1976–77—or even beyond.

It was just before Christmas—after a White House exercise in confusion and brinksmanship that kept American consumers and producers guessing till the last moment—that the doubts on the tax and energy bills were, as already noted, favorably resolved. Coupled with the easing of interest rates, these moves sent the stock market into orbit and caused a distinct brightening of the U.S. economic mood. But unemployment still hung high at 8 percent, and the vigor of the 1976 recovery was still a matter of dispute.

To those who expected continued huge economic slack, plus election-year politics, to generate a 1972-like letup in budgetary restraint, the hard line in the President's barrage of messages in January may have come as a surprise. But given President Ford's innate and consistent conservatism, and given the political threat of Ronald Reagan *from the right*, his proposal to cut back civilian services in pursuit of his twin-$28 billion tax and spending cuts was entirely predictable.

The essence of the President's fiscal program consisted of (1) a $20 billion cutback in the "current services budget" for fiscal 1977 (apparently, some $8 billion of the $28 billion cut demanded in October had evaporated in revisions of the numbers and congressional actions); (2) a continuation beyond July 1 of the temporarily extended $18 billion of income tax cuts; (3) a $10 billion further income tax cut, also as of July 1, for individuals and corporations (plus some minor tax "gimmicks" to stimulate investment by individuals); and (4) an increase in Social Security payroll taxes of $7 billion a year effective January 1, 1977.

Many economists felt that this was exactly the fiscal medicine the doctor had *not* ordered for the economy. My views on the matter were expressed as part of the following appraisal of the economic outlook and budget policy.

Ford's Budget and the Economy

THE WALL STREET JOURNAL *February 5, 1976*

Policy developments of the past few months have cleared the track for a respectable rate of recovery this year. Interest rates have backed down, the 1975 tax cuts have been extended, gradual rather than abrupt decontrol of oil prices is in prospect, and New York City has been pulled back from the brink of bankruptcy.

Rising business and consumer liquidity, ebbing inflation, accelerating retail sales, and a surging stock market all contribute to the atmosphere of expansion. All told, it is an encouraging backdrop for reaffirming the bullish forecast of a 7 percent advance in real GNP in 1976 that George Perry and I first ventured in October.

But President Ford's budget and economic policy messages cast an ominous shadow over late-1976 and 1977 economic prospects. His Economic Report resolves all economic doubts in favor of subdued expansion in 1976 lest we agitate the inflationary beast within us. And his budget sets the fiscal dials to "hard astern" for 1977. If Congress and the Federal Reserve respond with fiscal and monetary restriction this year, recovery could be imperiled next year long before the country reaches anything resembling full prosperity.

So the outcome of the Bicentennial battle of the budget will have profound implications not only for social policy but for economic performance. Where are the battle lines drawn for fiscal 1977? Given increasing budgetary caution and discipline in Congress and a conservative but not Neanderthal President in the White House, one can safely say that the range of outcomes is not bounded by wild election-year spending on one hand and a $90 billion cut on the other. Much more likely—giving proper weight to the President's budget cutting initiatives (and veto powers) and the shift toward sobriety-in-spending in Congress, both reinforced by the public's antispending mood—is a battle arena bounded at the upper end by a maintenance-of-services or hold-the-line budget of $414 billion and at the lower end by the President's $20-billion-cutback budget of $394 billion.

When the President first proposed his 28–28 program last October, he was operating from a "current services budget" benchmark of $423 billion. But after downward revisions in the light of more accurate information and "congressional increases threatened but not passed," the figure was scaled down to $414 billion. [But later revisions raised the price tag on the current services budget to $422 billion.] That is the level of spending that would be required in fiscal 1977 (beginning Oct. 1, 1976) to maintain services and commitments at fiscal 1976 levels. Mr. Ford would whittle $20 billion off this revised "current-services budget" by holding social programs $10.5 billion below prevailing levels; civilian and military pay, $3.5 billion below; other defense, $1.5 billion; and "all other," $4.5 billion.

Another way of looking at the 1977 Ford economy-model budget is to compare it with "normal" budgetary growth. The $21 billion increase over the fiscal 1976 budget is just half the average increase of the three preceding years. (After factoring in the three months' hiatus—with its own "transition quarter" budget—before fiscal 1977 begins, the applicable rate of increase comes to only $17 billion.)

Some $15 billion of the $21 billion increase represents the actual growth in defense and interest costs. This seems to leave only $6 billion for all other programs. But, as recovery continues, an added $5 billion becomes available through the automatic shrinkage of unemployment compensation and other "cyclical" transfer payments. Thus $11 billion is available to finance increases in all other "noncyclical" civilian programs. Normal growth in these programs, consisting of a 6 percent allowance for inflation and 4 percent real expansion, would come to $31 billion. By this measure, too, the Ford budget represents a $20 billion scaling back of government programs. So both the overall cutback and its impact on the level of social services are severe by any recent budgetary standards.

On the tax side, the President proposes extending the present $18 billion tax cut, plus another $10 billion cut in personal and corporate taxes effective July 1, 1976—all conditional on appropriate cuts in projected spending. His proposed increases in payroll taxes, effective next January 1, will offset nearly $7 billion (at annual rates) of the additional $10 billion.

The combined tax and spending changes in the Ford budget would add up to a withering fiscal drag on economic expansion during fiscal 1977. The high-employment surplus would rise by $19 billion for the fiscal year, with the restrictive pressure growing sharply and steadily during calendar 1977.

That the Congress will fully accept either the restrictive economic policy or the Spartan social policy implicit in Mr.

Ford's budget is highly unlikely. True, no spending spree is in prospect. But a reasonable working assumption is that the pulling and hauling on the budget will bring spending up to about $410 billion for fiscal 1977. And after another noisy struggle, a further extension of the present $18 billion cut seems to be a good bet.

This policy projection implies little fiscal constriction until after the election. But even if spending winds up at $410 billion, fiscal policy will tighten in fiscal 1977. The tightening will be very modest if the proposed income and payroll tax changes are not enacted. But if the payroll tax cuts are accepted while the added income tax cuts are rejected, the net result will be an $11 billion restrictive impact on a 1977 economy still operating far below reasonable target levels.

Monetary policy, after a year of puzzles and surprises, is even more difficult to sketch into the mosaic of the 1976 outlook. But a reasonable person, with fingers crossed, could assume that the Federal Reserve would not overreact to a strengthening recovery unless the inflation outlook suddenly darkens. In other words, a monetary policy that produces a mild rather than sharp rise in interest rates is a reasonable projection. This implies that short-term rates, after some further easing, will move up only moderately as the year progresses. Long-term rates are not likely to rise until later in the year, and then only after giving some further ground in the next few months, especially in the mortgage area.

Given only moderately accommodative fiscal and monetary policy for 1976, where do Perry and I find the expansionary strength to support a forecast of 7 percent real GNP growth? Primarily in a more upbeat view of consumption and business capital spending (and in the accompanying year-over-year advance of $25 billion in inventory investment) than most forecasters are projecting.

The sparkling performance of corporate profits will be the chief spur and lubricant for the revival of business fixed investment. Productivity advances and rising sales should generate a one-third rise in after-tax profits in 1976 on top of a striking jump during 1975. From 1975's first quarter to 1976's fourth, they should rise from $60 billion to over $100 billion at annual rates.

In a little longer—and "quality-corrected"—perspective, the profits boom is even more impressive. After inventory valuation adjustment (IVA)—that is, allowing for inventory replacement at current prices—profits in 1976 will be half again as high as in 1974. This will go a long way toward restoring corporate profitability, which had hit a postwar low of 8.1 percent of corporate product in 1974.

Led by the profit surge, internal cash flow this year will reach historically high levels relative to business fixed investment. Add to this the incentive of a more generous investment credit and the ability to draw on reinvigorated capital markets, and upward revisions of capital spending plans should be the order of the day. They are not yet reflected in plant and equipment surveys and capital appropriations. But the sensitive index of capital goods orders has been rising impressively since April. An "optimistic-realistic" expectation for this year, then, is an 11 percent rise in business fixed investment. Barring unexpected setbacks in the consumer sector, this advance should accelerate during 1976 and into 1977 and become a primary driving force for expansion.

The rise in consumer spending that started after the first quarter of 1975, stimulated first by tax reductions and then by rising payrolls, will continue during 1976 in response to (1) a continued rise in real disposable income as employment rises and wage gains outpace the inflation in living costs, (2) an improved consumer buying mood as buying power grows and the threat of layoffs recedes, (3) stock market advances and the rising backlog of demand for durable goods and (4) strengthened consumer liquidity growing out of a $100 billion-plus rise in consumers' liquid assets for 1975, together with only modest increases in installment debt. A rise of 11.5 percent in overall consumption—with autos and other durables as the star performers—is in the cards.

Housing at 1.5 million starts, a moderately declining net export balance, and a lackluster government sector—especially at the state-local level—round out the 1976 prospects. It all adds up to a 1976 GNP advance of $196 billion, to a total of $1,695 billion (using the new Commerce Department GNP benchmarks). For the first time in four years and only the second time since 1968, more than half of the advance will represent a real gain, less than half, inflation.

Inflation will continue to moderate in 1976. With a good 1975 harvest in hand and average crude oil prices scheduled to come down moderately, neither food nor fuel should add materially to the rate of inflation this year. And although rising demand will generate some added pressures on raw materials prices and on price margins, the moderate pace of recovery in the industrial world in 1976, coupled with pervasive slack in the U.S. economy, should hold these pressures in check this year. Thus the crux of the matter is the behavior of wage costs.

With 4½ million workers involved in major wage negotiations this year, the outcome will be crucial in determining price performance in 1976 and the later 1970's. As a result of cost-of-living escalators, several of the unions involved in the forthcoming negotiations have enjoyed wage advances considerably above the economy-wide average. If the government could influence these negotiations to set a pattern of moderation, the national goal of slowing the rate of inflation would be well served. These settlements would be a logical place to begin a gradual unwinding of the wage-wage and price-wage spirals. A reasonable expectation—even assuming that the big contracts, front-loaded as usual, will average 10 percent in the first year—is that economy-wide compensation per man-hour will rise about 8 percent this year.

Given the abatement of food and fuel inflation, the modest impact of demand pressures, and an 8 percent average pay increase, the rise in the GNP price deflator this year should ease to about 5¾ percent, or three points less than last year.

An inflation rate of less than 6 percent, coupled with a 7 percent advance in real output, is cause for considerable satisfaction but no complacency. Despite the above-trend gain in output, the end of the year will still see recession-like levels of unemployment, at 7¼ percent; of capacity utilization rates in manufacturing, at about 80 percent; and of economic slack, with actual output still running nearly $125 billion below the economy's potential (as measured at 5 percent unemployment).

Where lies fiscal responsibility in the face of such economic facts? Congress rightly prides itself on its more prudent fiscal posture and procedures. But if the new politics of fiscal responsibility, or austerity, simply leads to budget parsimony and willy-nilly economic restraint, its benefits will be swamped by its costs. Congress should vividly bear in mind that massive swings toward fiscal restraint in 1959–60 and 1974–75 exacted a huge toll in lost jobs and output.

To hit the fiscal brakes, as Mr. Ford proposes, when unemployment and economic slack are still legion and inflation is ebbing would be fiscally irresponsible. "Fiscal responsibility" is not synonymous with "fiscal restraint." Rather, it calls for an intelligent fitting of tax and spending positions to the needs of the economy. With its new budget procedures and staff, the Congress is now equipped to do this. Given the will, it can become a major force in effecting a new fiscal policy of responsible net stimulus in a lagging or sagging economy, and responsible net restraint in a prosperous but inflation-prone economy.

The foregoing article refers to "the shift toward sobriety-in-spending in Congress." Just as 1976 promised to be an atypical election year in terms of White House spending initiatives, no break-out of spending was likely to come from a Congress operating with new self-restraint under the 1974 Budgetary Reform Act. To be sure, the President did not spare the rhetoric about "election-year pork-barrel spending" in his February veto of the $6 billion jobs bill—but even that bill was carefully designed (a) to create jobs via public service employment, antirecession grants to state-local governments, and selected public works, and (b) to fit within the congressional budget ceiling set for fiscal 1976.

The new congressional sensitivity on spending and its expression in greater budget restraint rose out of an unusual convergence of (a) rising public resentment against federal spending, a mood aided and abetted by the Nixon-Ford-Simon rhetoric and policies, and (b) the fruition of long years of dogged efforts in Congress to reform and strengthen its budgetary processes and capabilities.

Before 1975, the "congressional budget" was nothing more than the sum of the individual appropriations for the various government functions and departments. Congress and its committees dealt with the left hind leg of the horse, its nose, its withers, its tail, but never the whole horse—and the budgetary animal that emerged often looked more like a camel. But now, the 1974 Act seemed to be taking hold.

Even before the procedure became mandatory, the Congress operated in 1975 under the new requirement that overall budget ceilings be set in spring and fall on the basis of careful congressional staff analysis and of recommendations by the new Senate and House Budget Committees. If the 1976 election-year handling of the budget hewed to this procedure—as it gave promise of doing—it was fair to say that congressional budgeting was well on its way through a significant watershed. Indeed, it seemed to be one of those striking instances of a change in *procedure* leading to significant changes in *substance*.

The public's general interest in curtailing government spending now had a vehicle for expression as a counterforce to the special-interest pressures for enlarging expenditures. Insofar as tighter procedures and better staffing through the new Congressional Budget Office led to better choices and better allocation of funds, this was all to the good. But for at least a minority of observers, it left this nagging question: Could the counterforce become so strong as to create a built-in bias *against* public spending as such?

I had this question very much in mind in testifying before the Joint Economic Committee early in February. After briefly presenting the essence of the economic forecast put forth in the foregoing *Wall Street Journal* article, the testimony dealt with policy matters and a growing concern over public misunderstanding on many budgetary and economic issues. The following excerpts from "Economic Policy and a Misguided Public" focus on the second part of the testimony.

Economic Policy and a Misguided Public

OPENING STATEMENT BEFORE THE JOINT ECONOMIC
COMMITTEE, U.S. CONGRESS *February 6, 1976*

Policy Considerations

If the President's budget and tax proposals were enacted, the recovery would be dealt a severe blow. The high-employment surplus would rise by $19 billion for the fiscal year 1977, a shift that masks a much bigger swing *during* 1976–77—a $30 billion jump in fiscal restriction from the spring of 1976 to the summer of 1977.A more prudent course would be to follow monetary and fiscal policies that will step up the rate of expansion in 1976 and continue it in 1977 until the corrosive waste of human and material resources has been brought back within tolerable bounds. Let me suggest several components of such a policy.

1. The Congress should put Mr. Ford's budget on the course of economic, social, and political responsibility. It would be well within that course to bring budget spending at least up to a maintenance-of-services level of $414 billion. Indeed, the analysis by Alice Rivlin, head of the Congressional Budget Office, puts the "baseline budget" at $425 billion, $31 billion above Ford's fiscal-

squeeze budget. Perhaps Congress will want to put more tax cuts and less spending in the economic mix than I might prefer. But, one way or another, it must overcome the huge swing toward economic restriction.

2. The Congress should do what it can to prevent monetary policy from swinging toward restriction long before high employment and full prosperity are within striking distance. I find it passing strange that the Federal Reserve—whose Chairman has not been bashful in making known his distaste for monetarist formulas—and the congressional banking committees—whose objectives would be far better served by emphasis on moderate levels of interest rates than by lock-step limits on money supply increases—should have coalesced on monetary policy targets stated exclusively in money supply terms. As the House Banking and Currency Committee, and especially Chairman Henry Reuss, have increasingly been urging, interest rates should be brought back into their proper place in setting policy targets.

3. Social Security payroll tax increases are the wrong medicine at the wrong place and at the wrong time. It seems particularly paradoxical to consider further cuts in the income tax, our best tax, at the same time that we would boost the payroll tax, which bears hard on the poor, raises business costs, and boosts the cost of living. With contingency reserves of over $40 billion, the Social Security System is in no immediate need of added revenues. And when that need materializes, it is high time to supplement the resources of the System with general revenues rather than cutting income taxes while boosting payroll taxes.

4. On income taxes, an adjustment of the proposed cuts to maintain the credits and tax breaks for the lowest income groups—who are still at the bottom of a very deep job barrel and have been hit hard by the amount and composition of inflation this time around—would be very much in order.

5. Finally, just a word on wage-price policy. Although it seems beyond the political pale in 1976, the Congress should never forget that a balanced program for full employment must contain some kind of restraint on excessive price increases exacted by concentrated industries and excessive wage increases exacted by overly powerful labor unions. Antitrust cannot cope with this problem. A more effective system of flagging down excessive wage and price increases in areas of the economy where competition is not an effective policeman must be part of a balanced program to overcome intolerable unemployment without incurring intolerable inflation.

The foregoing is obviously not meant to be a complete list. With some ingenuity, I am sure that it would be possible to develop an effective public service jobs program of about twice the present size (that is, to provide over 600,000 jobs) instead of phasing it out as Mr. Ford proposes. Also, in an economy still leagues away from excess aggregate demand, some public works step-up makes good sense. And the enormous pressure on state-local budgets suggests a generous program of antirecession grants, triggered to stay in effect only as long as unemployment is high and, by the same token, tilting the assistance toward the areas of highest unemployment.

To fight inflation, the Congress should be considering not only a moderate program of wage-price restraint in the areas of the economy that don't play the competitive game but also a de-escalation of regulations that prop up prices and costs. Innovative programs to trade off some reductions in payroll taxes in exchange for wage restraint and trade off grants to states in exchange for reductions of sales and excise taxes that boost the cost of living, should also get onto the congressional agenda.

Such long-run measures to cut the inflation rate are considerably more promising than the continued tight fiscal policy and threats of tight money that are the main weapons in the Administration's anti-inflation arsenal. Three points should be borne in mind by the Administration policy makers:

- They are fighting the war-before-last on inflation. They seem to forget what it took to give us that double-digit dose of inflation in 1973–74. There were five powerful engines of inflation: quintupling of oil prices, a 40 percent jump in food prices in 2½ years, double devaluation of the dollar, wage and price decontrol, and a worldwide commodity price boom. As these forces work their way through the economy, inflation is ebbing.
- If the Federal Reserve, after the constructive and stimulative easing of interest rates in the past few months, returns to aggressive tightening, it will be highly effective in choking down the rate of expansion but will have little effect on wage bargains, the decisions of Sheik Yamani and the Shah of Iran on oil prices, and drought or deluge in the Great Plains.
- Even without such sanctions as price suspension or rollback, the Council on Wage and Price Stability could have significantly more impact in restraining unwarranted price and wage increases if it had the obvious and enthusiastic backing of the White House and occasional access to the presidential pulpit.

The Misguiding of the American Public

I cannot conclude these remarks without expressing my growing concern over the distressing tendency in recent years to miseducate and, wittingly or unwittingly, mislead the American people on vital issues of economic policy and fact. This process, calculated or not, is contributing to misunderstanding of basic economic relationships, unnecessary anxiety on many fronts, and a loss of faith in the American economy and its public institutions. Let me cite a few examples.

The federal government is depicted as expanding like

some monstrous protoplasmic blob that threatens to snuff out economic freedom and initiative. Yet the facts will show that the federal budget as a proportion of GNP held in the neighborhood of 20 percent from 1953 to 1973. It is projected to rise to 22 percent in fiscal 1977—but adjusted to a full-employment basis, the figure would be right back at 20 percent.

Or take the supposed "crushing burden of federal debt." A striking chart included in last year's budget documents (but omitted this year) shows that the federal debt held by the public dropped from 83 percent of annual GNP in 1950 to 28 percent in 1976 (see chart 9). Seen in this perspective, the public debt is a far different and more

Chart 9. Federal Debt * as a Percent of GNP

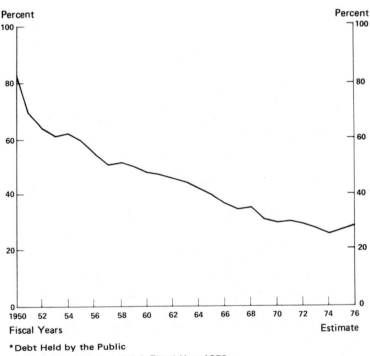

*Debt Held by the Public
Source: U.S. Budget in Brief, Fiscal Year 1976

manageable problem than the general impression abroad in the land.

A third area of widespread misapprehension centers on the large deficits in the federal budget. Here, two misimpressions are being fostered:

- The $70–75 billion deficit is being identified with profligacy in spending and fiscal irresponsibility when, in fact, it is almost entirely a hostage to recession. If we were operating at full employment, tax revenues would be about $50 billion higher than they are; unemployment compensation would be about $15 billion lower; and other cyclically-responsive outlays like food stamps, Medicare and Medicaid, and pensions, would be about $5 billion lower. So almost all of the deficit is a product of the recession. Ironically, the selfsame monetary and fiscal authorities whose disastrously tight policies in 1974 helped aggravate the recession and hence the deficit are the ones who are loudest in decrying it as an example of the lack of fiscal discipline.
- A related charge is that government deficits are the root of all inflationary evil. How is it, then, that inflation is ebbing in the face of the largest deficits in history?

A fourth area of anguished misapprehension relates to the Social Security System. The impression has been given that it is about to go broke. I need not tell this committee how far this is from the truth. Again, the recession is partly the culprit in cutting revenues and increasing the flow of benefits. The financing problems of the Social Security System can clearly be met.

A fifth example is the mistaken belief that Congress is an instrument of irresponsible and loose spending—an impression that totally ignores the responsible new procedures and spending limits that it is observing. It is disturbing in find how little awareness there seems to be around the country of the responsible way in which Congress is toeing the mark under its new budget reforms. Indeed, the greater danger at the moment in the light of the economy's needs is that there might be excessive zeal in clamping a ceiling on government expenditures.

Finally, the continuing barrage of statements and studies—for example, the April 1, 1975 release by the Treasury entitled "U.S. Ranking in Investment and in Real Economic Growth Is Among Lowest of Industrialized Countries"—is giving the public a false image of the true strength of the American economy. Only the "fine print" brings out that U.S. productivity is still the best in the world, with even the high-growth countries like France and West Germany having achieved only 80 percent of the American level of productivity.

Without being Pollyannas or burying their heads in the sand about persistent and troublesome economic problems, national leaders could in good grace put away their sackcloth and ashes and point with some pride to such comparative strengths of the U.S. economy as the following:

- As a First National City Bank study brings out, the United States has been growing steadily more competitive, with its unit labor costs rising only 10 percent from 1970 to 1974, while Canada's (with the next best performance) rose 29 percent, Germany's 90 percent, and Japan's 100 percent.
- Correspondingly, U.S. manufacturing exports held up remarkably well in the face of worldwide recession in 1975, and the U.S. dollar is still the most sought after currency in the world.

One hesitates to fix the blame for the retrograde movement in the economic education and knowledge of the American public. Much of it stems, as it has from time immemorial, from the self-serving efforts of particular groups to "sell" particular policies, positions, preferences, and prejudices. Note how many of these positions serve biases toward smaller government, toward cutbacks in federal spending, toward tax reductions for business and preferential tax treatment of capital investment, and toward restrictive fiscal and monetary policies.

To be candid about economic shortcomings and government problems is a virtue. But to denigrate the U.S. economy and exaggerate its problems and misidentify their
sources is certainly a vice. The sooner policy makers talk
economic sense instead of nonsense to the American people, the better our chances will be of coping with the truly
tough problems we face.

The Outlook

By 1976, some of the pressures on the economy, on
economists, and on economic policy makers were relent-
ing. The peak of inflation and the trough of recession were
past, and recovery was on schedule. The energy crisis had
turned from a sharp pain into a dull ache. New York, if not
back to health, was at least hobbling along on its crutches.
And internationally the new regimen of floating rates was
managing rather nicely.

Still, it was more a time of crises surmounted than of
problems solved. The Keynesian prescription of aggregate
demand stimulus was working rather well, spurring expansion without rekindling inflation. But prescribing suc-
cessfully for an economy that has caught the pneumonia
of deep recession remains far easier than curing the
chronic headache of too-high unemployment coupled with
too-high inflation. Once the economy's "buffer stocks" of
unemployment and idled industrial capacity are absorbed
by continued recovery, what is to protect us from resurg-
ing inflation?

Not that the inflation catapults of 1973–74—food shortages, the oil uprising, the commodity scramble, decontrol,
and devaluation—show any signs of being unlimbered
again. Even the fears of newly skyrocketing commodity
prices as the industrial economies again expand in tandem
seem to be overdone. A new study by Richard Cooper and
Robert Lawrence (published in *Brookings Papers,* 3:1975)
of the doubling of industrial commodity prices (other than

food and oil) from mid-1972 to mid-1974—which accounted for a quarter of world inflation in that period—traces a considerable part of that roaring price runup to "a whirlpool of speculation." Primary metals prices, for exmaple, rose 40 percent more than can be accounted for by historical relationships of prices to industrial production needs. The lesson for the future? Build up buffer stocks of strategic raw materials in slack times to throw into the speculative breach during the next commodity squeeze.

Analysis of the 1973–74 commodity price upsweep reminds us once more of how economists go about their business—in this case, isolating a specific form of the inflationary cancer, identifying its sources, and pinpointing a way of containing it. And it underscores also the vital need to disaggregate, to look at the structural micro-factors and forces that throw the macro-mechanism off balance, to look at the supply and price disturbances that disrupt aggregate demand management. The oil price explosion was only one example—albeit the most spectacular one—of sharp changes in supply prices that cause significant shifts in real income and purchasing power and require significant fiscal and monetary adjustments to compensate for the resulting effects on aggregate demand.

What inferences should the policy maker draw? First, that macro-policy will be open to disruption unless ways are found to protect its micro-flanks. Or, to put it differently, that demand management alone, relying on those buffer stocks of the jobless and excess capacity to contain inflation, is an inadequate answer in not only human but economic terms. Supply management—at this time, the building of buffer stocks of oil, food, and other strategic commodities—ought to be a basic ingredient of stabilization policy.

Second, economic policy will have to develop more delicate sensors and antennae as well as a more agile response mechanism, first, to minimize surprises and, second, to maximize the speed of response to external shocks and developing internal bottlenecks. Policy makers might still be surprised, but they would not, one hopes, be quite so dumbfounded.

The recent reform of the congressional budget process puts Congress in a new and better position to adapt its fiscal policy to changes in the economic environment. But further steps are required to lift and lengthen the sights of the political process by some more formal commitment to take the future into account. Whether this requires economic planning and programming on a national scale is an open question that the Humphrey-Javits and Humphrey-Hawkins bill and their backers in and out of Congress will keep very much alive. Out of the give-and-take on this issue, one may hope for at least a firm commitment by the White House and Congress to lengthen their perspective on economic policy—a resolve to draw on improved data, horizon-scanning, and future-focused analysis for earlier detection of emerging economic trends, threats of shortages, and danger signs in both the national and international economy.

Just as the economic future should not be left to chance, the coordination of monetary and fiscal policy must no longer be a matter of caprice. This is not to say that the Federal Reserve—probably the most independent central bank in the world—should be subordinated to the White House. But somehow, through more conscious and constructive cooperation of the White House, Congress, and Fed, must come an improved policy mix, a better fit of monetary to fiscal policy.

Under present arragements, should the desire be, for example, to run a tougher fiscal policy and easier monetary policy—more deficits (or bigger surpluses) coupled with lower interest rates—in order to tilt expansion in the direction of greater capital investment, there is no machinery to insure such a result. Again, the new budget procedures are an important step toward the necessary congressional cohesion for economic *entente*—and perhaps even *détente*. It puts Congress in a stronger position to strike and carry out bargains with the Federal Reserve and the White House not just on expansionary or restrictive policy *per se*, but on the relative emphasis on consumption and investment and the policy mix needed to carry it out.

But no amount of improvement in structural or supply policy or in coordination of fiscal and monetary policy can surmount the abiding problem that confronts us all: how (a) to create the 12 million jobs required between now and 1980 to absorb both the stream of new entrants into the labor force and the huge pool of unemployed workers and (b) doing so without touching off a new demand inflation later in the 1970's. It cannot be done simply by pumping up the economy and assuming that the flow of demand will find its way neatly into the nooks and crannies and hollows where stubborn unemployment exists.

Policies for economic expansion via monetary-fiscal stimulus will have to be carefully coupled with structural policies to increase productivity, to remove regulatory road-blocks to competition and lower costs, to improve labor information and mobility, to train and upgrade the disadvantaged, and to tide the unemployed over with temporary jobs and retraining rather than transfer payments alone. But even with such skillful tailoring of policies, it will be difficult to keep the pressures of high aggregate demand from once again putting the price-wage and wage-wage spirals in motion before unemployment is brought down to tolerable levels.

The day when these pressures reappear may be distant—and absent the shocks of 1973–74, there is no reason to expect inflation to be as virulent as in that benighted period. But the ominous postwar uptilt of inflation was in clear evidence before 1973 and can hardly be said to have faded away in 1976 with inflation still at levels that represented "new highs" in the 1952–1972 period. To urge bolder policies to step up expansion and cut unemployment more quickly in 1976–77 is to claim only that such moves are consistent with moderating inflation in a slack economy, not that inflation has dropped to tolerable levels nor that it will hold still if the economy is pushed to the limits of its potential.

To claim that would be to deny that the "unstable triad"—(1) full employment, (2) price stability, and (3) full freedom of economic choice—still prevails. In the face of powerful producer groups—labor, business, farmers, and so on—no long-run policy can deliver both full employment and contain inflation without some curbing of price and wage appetites. Clearly, "disciplining" labor by high unemployment and management by shrunken markets has been progressively less effective in de-escalating wage and price advances. On both sides, there is enough clout, enough market power, to enforce income claims that add up to more than the total output pie at existing prices. And conventional price and wage policies relying on mark-up pricing and "fair" wages add to the downward rigidity of prices and wages.

How to moderate these claims without the harsh treatment of deep recession or prolonged stagnation remains an unanswered challenge to economic policy. Sweden has perhaps come closest to solving it in a democratic society—though not without a degree of planning and intervention that has been unacceptable in this country to date.

The challenge to ingenuity in the United States is to find a formula for lowering the norm for wage and price advances. Part of the answer, as repeatedly urged in this book, is to impose some guidelines and restraints on the unions and businesses that wield excessive market power. And the time to install such limited restraints is precisely when the economy is operating far below its output potential. Once it gets there, it is too late—only more onerous controls will then do the job.

In the grander design, an incomes policy must seek an economic disarmament agreement in which labor and management agree to settle for slower advances in *money* income in exchange for less inflation, that is, without sacrificing *real* income. To forge such a social contract—and to provide the tax or other inducements, especially to labor, to initiate and maintain it—is at best a difficult task. But unless ways are found to de-escalate income claims, the prospect of attaining full employment without either unacceptable rates of inflation or unwanted degrees of wage-price control will remain clouded.

The U.S. economy of the mid-seventies has enough leeway for expansion to permit a long advance toward our employment and output goals without a resurgence of inflation. And a combination of good analysis and good policy could achieve some significant advances in coping with inflationary threats. But without some bold political leadership, skilled economic management, and a dose of good luck, the country will again face hard choices and uncomfortable trade-offs between jobs, prices, and controls in the late 1970's.

Part II

WHAT'S RIGHT WITH ECONOMICS?

GOING AGAINST OUR CURRENT FASHION OF TELL-
ing the world what's wrong with economics, I offer a
modest contribution to the immodest subject of what's
right with economics—and, in particular, what's right
with economics as a guide to public policy. In doing so,
I won't ignore the dark side of the moon—indeed, I
can't, since I will deal in part with the bedeviling subject of inflation. But believing that it is at least as reasonable to judge a discipline by its successes as by its
failures, I intend to accentuate the positive.

167

I. The Critical Look Inward

In recent years economists have instead accentuated the negative. In good part, this has taken the becoming form of *mea culpa* or rather *nostra culpa*. We have, for example, readily confessed that the inflationary shocks of 1973–74 caught not just the economy but the economist by surprise. On this and other fronts, the chorus of self-criticism has risen to a new crescendo. It is almost as if we take pride in our humility. Nietzsche must have been thinking of economists when he observed that "he who despises himself nevertheless esteems himself as a self-despiser."

This is not to imply that economists' criticisms are all self-inflicted wounds. Far from it. Often, among our colleagues' favorite targets are the shortcomings of mainstream economics, the misuse of modern techniques, the fallacies of conventional wisdom—in each case, the target is not the critic's but his colleagues' brand of economics, not *mea culpa* but *eorum culpa*.

In any event, he who comes to praise economics risks being buried in the barrage of indictments that economists have brought against themselves and their brethren. Let me give you a sampling of some that will be ringing in my ears as I follow the parlous path of economic virtue.

Ceremonial occasions—presidential, memorial, or inaugural addresses—in particular seem to evoke musings on the troubled or even dismal state of our science. For the American Economic Association faithful, I need only recall John Kenneth Galbraith condemning neoclassical and neo-Keynesian economics for ignoring power—thus losing

Presidential address delivered at the eighty-eighth meeting of the American Economic Association, San Francisco, California, December 29, 1974. The address was abridged for oral delivery. I owe particular thanks for the many conversations I held with Francis M. Boddy, Otto Eckstein, Edward Foster, John R. Meyer, Arthur Okun, Joseph Pechman, George Perry, Robert Solow, and James Tobin. I also wish to thank Gardner Ackley, Kenneth Arrow, Walter P. Heller, Franco Modigliani, Alice Rivlin, Paul Samuelson, Charles Schultze, Christopher Sims, and George Stigler for contributions to the adult education that underlies this address. The errors, of course, are mine.

contact with the real world; Kenneth Boulding assailing welfare economics for its reliance on that holiest of holies, Pareto optimality—when in fact "our lives are dominated by precisely this interdependence of utility functions which the Paretian optimum denies"—thus losing contact with the real world; and Wassily Leontief attacking mathematical economics for building a showy superstructure on weak empirical foundations and unverified assumptions—thus losing contact with the real world.

In one form or another, variations on Leontief's lament have been heard in many another presidential address, to wit:

- By F. H. Hahn (Econometric Society, 1968), who decried "the spectacle of so many people refining the analysis of economic states which they give no reason to suppose will ever, or have ever, come about."

- By G. D. N. Worswick (Section F of the British Association, 1971), who viewed the performance of economics as "curiously disappointing," suggesting that it has "a marvelous array of pretend tools which would perform wonders if ever a set of facts should turn up in the right form."

- By E. H. Phelps Brown (Royal Economics Society, 1971), who judged the usefulness of current work in economics as "not equal to its distinction" because it is "built on assumptions about human behavior that are plucked from the air."

- By James H. Blackman (Southern Economic Association, 1971), who noted that models with sufficiently intriguing mathematical properties can achieve lives of their own even if they lead the investigator further away from reality and yet, "the profession's incentive system tends perversely to reward this kind of endeavor and to deflect the attention of gifted economists from the exploration of concrete problems and the dirty work that entails."

- By Sherman Maisel (American Finance Association,

1973), who concluded that most of the literature of monetary economics is "nonoperational" because (a) its prescriptions are too often based on limited or false assumptions, (b) it bypasses critical operational problems, and (c) it ascribes too great validity to its statistical tests.

- By Barbara Bergmann (Eastern Economic Association, 1974), who prefaced her plea for more microsimulation to incorporate "realistically messy information" in our economic data base with a few roundhouse swings at the economics profession and the pointed observation that instead of studying the real nature of decision-making, we typically rush to make assumptions "whose purpose in life is to let the theorem emerge, all neat and provable."

Another favorite line of criticism and attack focuses on the implicit value premises of conventional economics. Gunnar Myrdal and Robert Heilbroner chide us for concealing the value judgments that inevitably enter into our selection of problems for study, choice of approach, definition of concepts, and even gathering of data. So a "value-free" economics is an illusion—they urge economists to specify their values and thus avoid biases and make research more realistic.

Radical economists simply reject the whole value system of conventional economics—as they see it, the neoclassical paradigm in its very bone and marrow enthrones acquisitiveness and enshrines the existing order. Paul Sweezy accuses mainstream economists "of hiding the facts, of making the uncontrollable appear under control, of rationalizing a system which condemns hundreds of millions of people to lives of despair and starvation. . . ."

Inflation is the latest source of critical volleys, and I will get to these in due course. Meanwhile, the sampler of economic masochism I have already provided should serve as ample insurance against complacency or smugness in considering "what's right with economics." At the same time, it strongly suggests that economics, more than any other social science, is afflicted with the common scold.

I recognize that such a quick sampling and cryptic quotes, selected to highlight criticism, do a certain injustice to economics and to some of the quoted economists whose kindlier observations have been neglected in the process. But I am also aware that my litany omitted a number of familiar flaws, e.g., our impounding of tastes and preferences in *ceteris paribus;* the shortcomings of the maximization principle in explaining consumer and producer behavior, especially in the short run; and our limited ability to bring the claims of future generations into our social utility functions.

Were I to serve as defense counsel for the profession on this wide variety of indictments, I would urge that we plead guilty or take the Fifth on some, take to the defense on others, and take offense at the rest. Having paid my respects to the critics, I intend no point-by-point evaluation or rebuttal. This has been ably undertaken by others.* Rather, my object is to gain a more balanced perspective by focusing on the quality, role, and contributions of economics, especially to public policy. In that undertaking, the first step is to examine the flank we expose to the public.

II. *The Economist and the Public*

When we turn from inside to outside critics, the focus changes. We may think, rightly, that freely confessing our weaknesses and airing our differences stimulate responses and adaptations that strengthen economics. Yet, wearing our purple hearts on our sleeves has its price. It nourishes the darkest suspicions about our art and supplies live ammunition to outside critics who have declared open season

* Among those who have sprung to the defense with varying degrees of fervor are Harry Johnson (1968), Donald MacDougall (1974), Charles Schultze (1972), Robert Solow (1970, 1971), and James Tobin (1973, 1974). For more general appraisals of the criticisms and the state of economics, see Blackman (1971) and Nancy Ruggles (1970).

on economists. Witness the open sesame to the op-ed pages for such recent thrusts as Bergmann's assault on economists in general and Friedrich von Hayek's attack on Keynesians in particular. With everything from off-the-cuff phrases about being "caught with our parameters down" to tracts for the *Times*, we feed the hand that bites us.

This is not a plea to do our self-flagellating in secret or to mute our disputes and conflicts. Open controversies, openly arrived at, are part of the therapy that keeps our profession healthy. Rather, my plea is to the media and the opinion-makers to understand that appearances are deceiving, that hard give-and-take is indeed a symbol of strength, and that our areas of agreement and consensus are vastly larger than our areas of difference.

On the first point, observers from other disciplines are often astonished at how hard economists go at each other, how readily they run the gauntlet of their colleagues' criticisms with no quarter asked for and none given—and, with few exceptions, all this within the framework of professional respect and friendship. As Charles Frankel put it, unlike other social sciences, economics seems to have achieved "a working etiquette which allows people to disagree vigorously without engaging in recriminations about 'unscientific' or 'unprofessional' behavior" (quoted in Johnson [1973]).

What accounts for this? Part of it, one can unblushingly say, is simply that so many competent, tough, and rigorously trained minds have been drawn into economics in response not just to challenging policy problems but to the quantitative revolution since World War II. And part of it is that the participants can draw on a hard core of economic theory and methodology, together with a growing body of empirical knowledge, to provide standards for testing the validity (though not necessarily the relevance and reality) of ideas, analysis, and empirical findings. The result is not only a relentless intellectual policing of the profession that soon exposes the fool, the quack, and the charlatan, but a growing capacity "to participate in adversary debate over public policy issues without jeopardizing scientific integrity and freedom" (Johnson [1973]).

That brings me to the second point, the impression we give outsiders of a house divided, not to say splintered. It is worth reminding ourselves and our critics of several factors that drive a wedge between image and reality.

One, instead of laying aside our differences and living contentedly together, we economists tend to lay aside our agreements and live contentiously together. We focus our private and public debates on unsolved policy problems, tough analytical nuts, and issues on which we have rival theories, contradictory evidence, or strong ideological differences. Just as these are the questions that intrigue us, they are the ones that attract the attention of press and public. What we know—and they may not—is that under the visible tip of disagreement and rivalry lies no huge iceberg of divisiveness.

Two, it is only occasionally that our areas of consensus are brought to the surface in a newsworthy way. One such occasion was the White House "summit conference" on inflation in September 1974. Two dozen leading economists from across a wide spectrum of American economics (not wide enough, the radicals would say) signed a statement which called on President Ford and the Congress to eliminate twenty-two restrictive laws and practices that inhibit competition, inflate costs, and prop up prices. Only a tiny minority held out (if any minority that includes Galbraith can be called "tiny"). Even more striking, in a sense, was that while the customary and largely ideological clashes among, say, Galbraith, Milton Friedman, and Paul Samuelson caught the public eye, the real story lay in the minimal dissent among the participants on (a) the forecast of a soggy or sagging economy, (b) the urgency of providing relief to the victims of inflation and the casualties of recession, (c) the need to ease monetary restraint, (d) the small anti-inflationary payoff on moderate ($5–10 billion) budget cuts, and (e) the advisability of resisting popular demands for reimposing full-scale wage and price controls.

Three, even where disagreement flourishes—most visibly, perhaps, between Keynesians and monetarists—the public may not discern that the analytical and empirical ties that bind us are far stronger than the forces that divide us. Our controversies take place within the context of basic consensus on the nature and methods of economic theory and inquiry, on the content of the disagreement, and on the kinds of tests that may one day resolve the conflict. "Such disagreement within agreement lies at the heart of the process of normal development of a science" (Benjamin Ward [1972]).

Four, much of what the public perceives as a clash of economic concepts and findings is in fact a clash of ideology and values. Given the way technical economics and ethical preferences are packaged in policy debates (and given our lapses in identifying which is which), this is hardly surprising. Thus, whoever opens the package labeled "monetarist" typically finds not just money supply in full flower, but a dedication to minimum government intervention, small budgets, reliance on rules rather than authority, and price stability. Contrasting correlations appear in the Keynesian package. So outsiders can be excused for slipping into the fallacy of association and attributing the split to our unresolved analytical conflicts rather than to divergent evaluations of social priorities and competing philosophies of government. These associational chains are not linked together by any inexorable logic—in part, they seem to be an accident of birth as in the case of the Chicago twins of monetarism and *laissez-faire* rules. A belief in the supremacy of monetary over fiscal tools could quite logically go hand-in-hand with avid interventionism. But this escapes the jaundiced eye of the outside observer, who takes the ideological lineup as further evidence that economics is riven to its core.

Five, there is an ironic but substantial inverse correlation between the degree of consensus among economists and the degree of public acceptance of their findings. Thus, in the macroeconomic sphere of stabilization policy, where debate and disputes among economists flourish, their imprint on public policy is undeniable. But in the considerably more peaceful realm of microeconomics and allocative efficiency—where a reliable analytical apparatus coupled with solid quantitative work, especially on costs and benefits, has led the great majority of disinterested economists to an agreed diagnosis and prescription—the policy boxscore shows few hits, fewer runs, and lots of runners left on base. Economists widely, in some cases almost uniformly, favor tougher antitrust policy, freer trade, deregulation of transportation, pollution taxes in place of most prohibitions, and tax reform to remove income tax shelters. They oppose fair trade laws, restrictive labor and management practices, distortive zoning laws and building codes, import quotas, ceilings on interest rates, maritime subsidies, and pure (or impure) pork barrel projects.

Granted, the diffuse and inchoate consumer interest has been no match for the sharply focused, articulate, and well-financed efforts of producer groups. But the economist is beginning to pick up some allies. Public interest groups are increasingly giving focus and force to the consumer and general public interest. And the march of events is providing some windfalls: Among the apples that have dropped in our laps are flexible exchange rates, the dethroning of agricultural price supports, inroads on import quotas, and moves to end percentage depletion for oil and gas. Under the pressure of virulent inflation, government actions that erode productivity and boost costs and prices are being subjected to new and searching scrutiny. So perhaps, on these microeconomic issues where economists sing in reasonably close harmony, the outside world will no longer quite tune us out. In macroeconomic policy, where cacophony prevails, we can be sure that the world will tune us in.

It may also be useful to draw attention—especially the attention of those that interpret us to the public—to certain other misperceptions and roadblocks that thwart good economics and tend to put economists in bad repute.

First, much of our economic analysis and the uncommon sense growing out of it fly in the face of "common sense"; for example: that budget deficits need not spell inflation, nor national debt a burden on our grandchildren; that thriftiness can be a mixed virtue; that while exploding oil prices *in*flate costs, they *de*flate demand; that in an overheated economy, greater taxes can be the lesser evil; and so on. Behind every false dictate of common sense lies a primitive and misbegotten economic theory— and for most of our pains to correct it, we can expect to get the back of everyman's hand.

Second, a related cross to bear can be characterized by Kermit Gordon's apt phrase, "virtue is so much easier when duty and self-interest coincide." Not only does that foredoom action on many microeconomic fronts, as already noted, but it puts roadblocks in the path of efforts to make fiscal policy a two-way street. For forty years, Congress has enacted major tax increases only under the whiplash of war. The resulting reliance on tight money to fight peacetime excess demand, coupled with expansionary fiscal policy to fight recession and slack, have had an unmistakable ratchet effect that has tilted the system toward tighter money and easier budgets. (Small wonder, by the way, that many economists and policy makers are unwilling to give up, via indexing, the increases in effective income tax rates "legislated" by inflation.)

Third, the public sees economists as bearers of hard and unpalatable truths. And often we are, by the very nature of our sometimes dismal discipline. Except when idle resources can be put to work or productivity increased, our message is the stern one of trade-offs, benefits at a cost, and no one-dimensional daydreaming. Even worse, at times economics has to bring the bad tidings that for some problems there are no satisfactory solutions. For some thirty years, we have warned that full employment, price stability, and full freedom of economic choice cannot coexist in a world of strongly organized producer groups. More recently, economic analysis has brought home the unromantic truth that failure to cure some of our social ills traces less to a failure of will, or "right-wing villains," or a calloused "establishment," or powerlessness of the people than it does to the prosaic facts that the problems are tough and complex and the goals we seek may be irreconcilable—in short, traces more to conflicts in our national objectives than to conflicts among social groups. Welfare reform is a case in point: no solution can simultaneously provide a decent minimum income for all, preserve work incentives, cut no one's benefits, and avoid huge budget costs (Schultze [1972]; Rivlin [1973]). We as economists may view such work as a contribution to straight thinking and rational choice. Our critics are more likely to view it, at worst, as a counsel of defeat (which it is not) or at best a counsel of inescapable compromise (which it is).

Since the foregoing misperceptions and roadblocks thwart the translation of good economics into good policy, one could justify, in cold cost-benefit terms, a sizable investment to overcome or reduce them. The most obvious implication is that the country needs to invest more in formal economic education at all levels. But an equally pressing need is for economists to invest more of their time and effort in making themselves understood to the public and policy maker—and that in turn requires recognition of this skill in the academic reward system. This might serve as a useful antidote to the influence of mathematics and econometrics which, while heightening the precision of professional thinking and internal communication, have apparently dulled the appetite and eroded the facility to communicate with the public in intelligible English prose.

In a very real sense, this confronts the press with an unusual opportunity and challenge, perhaps even a responsibility, to serve as a translator and interpreter of economics and its offerings. But believing (probably rightly) that their readers and listeners prefer to hear of fights and failures, crises and controversies, rather than of quiet contributions and consensus, the conventional or electronic press is not very likely to rise to this challenge. So it is still up to economists.

III. Standards of Judgment

From the foregoing, it is evident that I feel, first, that economists have gone beyond beguiling humility and welcome self-criticism to the point of almost neurotic self-rebuke and, second, that press and public have all too lustily taken up the cry—in part taking us at our word, in part misinterpreting us, and in part reflecting their belief that, after the high promise of the 1960's, we have failed them in not foreseeing and forestalling the crises of the 1970's: stagflation, energy shortage, and the environment.

In my quest for a more balanced perspective on the state of economics, the next task is to set up some standards for judging the quality and performance of economists. Since we have developed no measures of output or allocative efficiency, no capital-output or cost-benefit ratios, for the economics "industry," I will have to fall back on more subjective and less quantitative measures in judging its quality and contributions.

My mixed bag of criteria includes (1) the quality of inputs; (2) the demands for our services; (3) as a proxy for a measure of outputs, the record of accomplishment in a given field (public finance); (4) finally, the cruelest test, our handling of the economics of inflation.

The potential of economics for informing and improving public policy depends on the stock of human capital, technology, and tools at its command. Here, economics has no difficulty in holding its head high, especially in terms of the striking advances of the past three or four decades. Harry Johnson may be a trifle extravagant in his assessment that the United States now has "perhaps fifty economic departments of an average quality comparable to the average quality of the four or five best departments in the whole world in the pre-World War II period"—but only a trifle (Johnson [1973]).

Accompanying the growth in the quantity and quality of economic brainpower have been striking advances in the techniques and tools with which economists work. One need only consider the strengthened analytical base of micro- and macroeconomics; the methodological revolution that moved us from the rationalist-historical approach into the age of quantification, with its insistence on systematic measurement of the shapes of economic functions and empirical testing of hypotheses and its use of econometrics and simulation techniques (with a powerful assist from the computer); and such conceptual advances as those in the economics of human capital, of cost-benefit relations, of uncertainty, of control, of transactions and information costs, of "second best," and of the allocation of time.

In normative economics and the analysis of value-laden social problems, new frontiers in the study of economic behavior are being opened up by survey research techniques (especially by the Michigan Survey Research Center), by efforts to measure nonmarket benefits or values (especially by the National Bureau of Economic Research) and by "controlled" social experimentation (for example, by the Brookings Institution and the University of Wisconsin Institute for Research on Poverty). These newer tools and the institutions that nurture them constitute part of the rich and expanding resources of economics.

Economics can also draw on a broad data base, especially in federal statistics. But here, the quantity, timeliness, and even the quality of the data are not keeping pace with either the problems requiring analysis or the capacity of our quantitative techniques. Responding to policy needs and mounting self-criticism, the profession has opened many new fronts in the search for realistic microdata to link up with macrodata, for cross-section data to help overcome the curse of collinearity in time series analysis, and for custom-built data developed by survey and experimental techniques.

That the human, analytical, and quantitative resources of economics provide a huge potential for solving problems seems undeniable. That more of these powerful resources than ever before are being put at the disposal of economic policy makers also seems undeniable. What we do not know is what proportion is being misdirected into arid puzzles, sterile proofs, and recreational mathematics while the world's pressing economic and social problems go begging for answers. Here, we can only match one observer's impression against another. The profession itself has not come to grips with *this* question of allocative efficiency.

A second test in appraising the state of economics, one not unknown to economics, is that of the marketplace. This takes several forms, none very robust, but none trivial. The first is the recent upsurge in enrollments in economics courses—especially in introductory courses. The second is the oft-reported high ranking of economists' salaries in business, government, and academic life. A third is the strong and growing demand for economists' inputs into the policy-making process—either as staff members or as expert witnesses for congressional committees, individual Congressmen, and the executive branch.

With students, business, and government beating a path to our door, we can infer that something must be right with economics, or wrong with the economy, or both. Either we are building a better mousetrap or there are more and bigger mice threatening our customers. Perhaps it is simply that we have the only mousetraps in town.

But there must be more to it than that. Take the policy maker, for example. What he finds congenial is that he can hand an economist a problem—relating to changes in taxation, regulations, budget proposals, pollution control, poverty, social security, public service jobs, gasoline taxes, oil prices, and so on—and be reasonably sure of getting a useful appraisal of alternative paths to his objectives, of costs and benefits, and of distributional, allocative, and stabilization impacts. Many of these judgments will come with orders of magnitude or reasonably precise numbers attached. He may not trust our GNP forecasts, but he has come to respect our hardheaded analysis and numbers on the myriad problems of economic choice with which he is faced.

It seems fair to draw another inference: notwithstanding the current wave of self-criticism and public criticism, even lampooning, of economists and despite our highly visible public debates and highly vulnerable participation in policy-making, economics continues to maintain its standing as a science. Signs of a reported crisis of public confidence or of a "recession of self-confidence" are few and far between. Reports of the demise of our discipline are grossly exaggerated.

IV. The "Outputs" of Public Economics

Having considered some indicators of the quality of our inputs and of the revealed preferences for our outputs, let me continue this exercise in casual (and congenial) empiricism by taking an unscientific but not unrepresentative sample of the outputs of economics, especially those bearing on policy. For this purpose, I draw on my chosen field of public finance, or public economics, to illustrate the telling conceptual and empirical advances of economics in recent decades and the resulting enrichment of its offerings to the policy maker.*

PUBLIC EXPENDITURES

Consider first the striking contributions economics has made in the past generation to clear thinking and better informed decisions on public expenditures. Partly, this reflects advances in economic science, e.g., in the theory of public goods and human capital, and partly, creative new applications of the economist's characteristic way of looking at problems of choice, namely, through the lens of op-

---

* See in this connection Alan S. Blinder and Robert M. Solow, et al. This is the capstone volume of the Brookings Studies on Government Finance, directed by Joseph A. Pechman. See also Carl S. Shoup, et al.

portunity cost, benefits, and alternative paths to a stated goal.

Economics can offer much more concrete guidance on efficient ways of allocating resources to achieve stated governmental objectives than it can on what the public-private sector division of resources should be. That may be a good thing in that presidents and Congressmen view the fixing of goals for public health, housing, welfare, and the like as what *they* were elected for, yet at the same time seek, or at least accept, economic guidance on the choice among competing methods of achieving these goals.

Nonetheless, rapid progress in the theory of public goods since the appearance of the Samuelson classic on "The Pure Theory of Public Expenditures" just twenty years ago has vastly improved on the simplistic theory it replaced. (Samuelson, 1954) It has facilitated straight thinking, first, on the derivation of conditions for efficient public-sector allocations from private evaluations and, second, on the articulation of social priorities through the political process.

Interwoven with the newer thinking about public goods has been a resurgent interest in externalities or spillover effects. In a sense, the pure collective good is a case of total externality—all of its benefits are external and non-marketable since nobody can be excluded from them. That may clarify thinking but gives little policy guidance.

Yet the externality concept translates into hard-headed policy advice in such disparate areas as pollution, federal aid, and the law. When pollution became a national concern, economists quickly drew on their tool kit to develop proposals for antipollution taxes (within the context of target air and water quality standards). Tax penalties of so much per unit would put price tags on use of the public's air and water, thus internalizing external costs and using market incentives to accomplish depollution rather than relying on the less efficient route of regulation.

When local governments supply education and public health services to a mobile population, many of the benefits spill over to other units. An important rationale for federal grants flows from these externalities, namely, that to get local units to produce enough education and health service to achieve a national, not just a local, cost-benefit optimum requires conditional grants from the federal purse.

Further, since externalities in the form of damage to third parties lie at the heart of many problems in legal justice, economics is able to make an important contribution in this area.

When we turn to the empirical outputs that are now illuminating problems of public choice, we find the past decade bristling with new thinking, new techniques, and new measurements. These offer the decision-maker important new guides in the selection and evaluation of government programs and new insights into alternative systems of delivering government services:

• Measurement of cost-benefit ratios has developed from the early metrics of water projects into, first, a sophisticated cost-benefit calculus for tangible investments like dams, roads, pollution-control projects and, second, cost-benefit estimates for intangible investments in human brainpower, skills, and health. Shadow pricing has been one of the useful tools in this connection. Cost-benefit analysis, even with its limits of quantification and its inability to shed light on distributional and value questions, is an important aid to informed decisions.

• A related advance is the development of new and tougher standards for judging government programs. The former criteria centered on the question: Is the program put into effect quickly and with high fidelity to the congressional intent? Now, the accountability question is: Does it deliver the goods? Does it accomplish the objectives? Inputs used to be stressed—if they conformed with the intent of the legislation, they tended to be judged a success. But now we try to measure outputs, a tougher and more elusive standard. (The parallel with judging the performance of economics and economists is painfully obvious.) Antipoverty programs, which were among the first to be evaluated by these stringent standards, seem to have borne the brunt of the evaluation boom. By the old inputs standard, a program like Head Start would have fared much better.

• The reach of cost-benefit analysis will be lengthened if a broad range of new research efforts in nonmarket sectors of economic activity pays off. I refer not only to the exciting work on measurement of the returns on investments in human capital (T. W. Schultz), but to efforts to measure the output of the medical industry, to measure the relations between crime and punishment, and to measure the value of nonmarket economic activity conducted *within* firms and households.

• The new technique of controlled social experimentation on proposed welfare and housing measures, health insurance, and education vouchers is yielding important insights (Rivlin [1973]). As a result of experiments on negative income taxation in New Jersey, for example, the equity-versus-efficiency, or equality-versus-incentives, controversy will never be conducted in a vacuum again. In spite of some limitations, the New Jersey experiment yielded strong evidence that fears of fatal incentive effects of a negative income tax were grossly overblown.

• Another focus of fruitful thinking relates to alternative strategies for delivering social services. The in-cash versus in-kind choice is a basic one. Economists are predisposed toward the in-cash approach on grounds that one can generally depend on people to follow their own best interests. But there are significant exceptions where consumer sovereignty is limited or specific goods externalities exist or some explicit social values take priority.

• Out of economics also comes the attempt to develop "market analogs" to serve as substitutes for market incentives in reconciling public with private interests, decentralized individual decisions with social goals (Schultze [1971]). Pollution taxes are a case in point. Performance standards for teacher pay would be another. Putting medical insurance programs on an efficiency-based reimbursement basis would be a third. The big gap is in the redesign of incentives and institutions to guide decentralized government decision-making more systematically toward the aims of our social programs. Thus far, the government, like the economics profession, is largely in the dark about its own production function.

TAXATION

What strikes an old public finance functionary as forcibly as any change in the field of public finance is the way in which modern thinking has knocked the props out from under the neat and primitive theories of tax incidence of a generation ago. The property tax on housing serves as an instructive case in point. The textbooks of the 1930's and 1940's told us confidently that the tax on land (fixed supply) was capitalized and on dwellings (supply-responsive) fell like an excise tax on the occupant, the consumer of housing services. The policy lesson was clear: Given the declining proportion of income spent on housing services as income rises, the tax was hopelessly regressive. Today? It is recognized that the old incidence analysis was wrong, even on its own terms.

The modern theory of incidence (defined as the impact on distribution of private real income) draws on general equilibrium theory, distinguishes between sources-of-income and uses-of-income effects, and disentangles the concepts of specific, differential, and balanced-budget incidence. The resulting analysis indicates that much of the aggregate burden of the property tax falls on owners of capital and hence tends to be progressive—and this progressivity is enhanced by the particular "excise-type" effects of this tax (Aaron [1974]). In short, error has been exposed and though the debate is not over, we are now in transit toward truth.* It is hard to put down the knee-jerk reaction that prefixes "property tax" with "regressive." And it will take some time before policy makers accept the proposition that, at the very least, the property tax is now in the unexpected position of "innocent until proved guilty." But the implications for policy are profound.

Economists have long been useful and influential contributors to the design of the federal tax structure and of particular taxes. Again, elementary concepts we now take for granted—for example, horizontal versus vertical equity, Richard Musgrave's three branches of distribution, allocation, and stabilization, the lagged effect of tax changes, and automatic versus discretionary tax changes—were not even part of our vocabulary in the pre-World War II period. Yet, all of these are now factored into our economic advice on taxation.

Even more directly impinging on policy are the empirical advances. One thinks of searching studies of particular taxes and tax components (especially in the Brookings Studies on Government Finance), and of the relentless identifying and quantifying of federal income tax preferences or "loopholes." Much of the thrust of economists' recent work on these "tax expenditures" has been (a) to identify the beneficiaries and specify the size of the government subsidies provided in the form of preferential tax treatment, (b) to define the inequities, both horizontal and vertical, that they create, and (c) to estimate the distortions in resource flows caused by preferential treatment of oil and gas, housing, real estate partnerships, and the like and measure the resulting welfare loss. Though the congressional response has been slow and halting, progress has been made along the lines plotted by economists, and

---

* Those who view decisions to locate in a particular community as a conscious choice of one particular bundle of public services over others conclude that the property tax on housing is a benefit tax, a payment for benefits received.

a solid base has been laid for the further tax reform that is surely coming.

Out of the countless other advances, one stands out, namely, the highly informative work done on the distributional impacts of taxation with the aid of the powerful tool of micro-unit data files (for example, the MERGE file developed by Joseph Pechman and Benjamin Okner). Such micro-unit files are a new-generation statistical missile, MIRVed so that they can simultaneously hit multiple revenue-estimating and burden-distribution targets. With their help, for example, economists have measured the growing burden of income, payroll, and consumption taxes on the lower income groups and developed techniques for removing them—most recently, in the context of the impact of inflation on the same groups.

One should add that if revolution rather than reform becomes the order of the day in the federal tax structure, the economist is ever ready with reasonably sophisticated analytics and a fair amount of empirical information on such major alternatives as a value-added tax, a progressive expenditure tax, and a net-worth tax. One of the next stages in tax research, a highly complex one, will be the general equilibrium analysis of such sweeping changes in the tax system as, say, the substitution of a value-added tax for the corporate income tax or for part of the payroll tax. Or, if stimulation of private saving becomes a compelling objective, perhaps the substitution of an expenditure tax for part of the income tax will become a live issue. The skills of the economist will be front and center in any such redesign of the tax system.

The negative income tax story is relevant here. The concept and its rudimentary principles were developed and discussed among economists in the early 1940's. Some of us were already using it as a teaching device in the mid-1940's. A quarter-century after its origin, it became the basis for the Family Assistance Plan developed by Mr. Nixon's economists. And a more limited version of the plan seems again to be rustling in the leaves.

FISCAL POLICY

In the domain of fiscal policy, it is harder to answer the question, "What have you economists done for us lately?" with a sparkling array of examples. Much of the theoretical ferment in this field is associated with the flowering of Keynesian macroeconomics in the late 1930's and 1940's, the very period when the microeconomics of tax incidence and public expenditures languished.

Conceptual advances have continued throughout the past 25 years, but they have been more in the nature of a fleshing out and consolidation of the original breakthroughs with the aid of the powerful tools of mathematics and econometrics. Multiplier analysis, for example, has moved from the theoretical realm into large computer models of the economy—with the tax cut of 1964 and the surtax of 1968 providing empirical grist for the mill. While the models differ on the exact value of the multiplier, "a fiscal policy planner will not often be led astray if he uses a multiplier of 2" for government spending. (Blinder and Solow [1974])

Coupled with multiplier studies is the even more subtle study of the structure of the "outside lags," of the timing of responses in the economy to changes in fiscal policy. Though the empirical efforts and debates go on apace, the behavior of the cumulative multipliers in a clutch of economic models suggests that for any given change in fiscal policy, "at least 75 percent, probably much more, of the ultimate effect is felt within the first year after the initiation of the policy." (Blinder and Solow [1974])

Although intractable questions remain concerning investment responses to fiscal policy changes, enough has been learned about aggregate demand responses to provide two broad generalizations about fiscal policy:

- One, the conditions for intelligent fiscal policy decisions are met if economic forecasting can answer two not-very-exacting questions: Do projected economic conditions in the ensuing six to nine months call for restraint or stimulus? Is the required dosage large or small?

- Two, given the limited margin for error in a high-employment economy, it is better to rely on many smaller monetary-fiscal moves than a few large ones.

Implicit in these two generalizations is a third one: Given both the internal shifts and the external shocks with which stabilization policy has to cope, a discretionary policy that makes efficient use of feedback information will be more effective than an automatic policy that locks in on fixed fiscal and monetary targets.

Development of a simplified measure of fiscal impact revolving around the "full-employment surplus" concept is another example of the typical process by which economists expose error, develop approximations of truth, but continue the vigorous debate on further improvements. First, policy makers had to be weaned away from the annually balanced budget and the cyclically balanced budget as policy targets and from actual deficits or surpluses (especially in budgets other than the national-income-accounts budget) as measures of budget stimulus or restriction. It was not easy. It took almost a quarter of a century before a Democratic president was converted (in 1961) and another decade to capture a Republican White House.

But success on the policy frontier has its own pitfalls, both political and economic. What was intended as a measure of policy was instead taken as a goal, namely, a balanced budget at full employment, a "self-fulfilling prophecy" as the Nixon Administration called it. This erroneously implied that the fiscal target should remain fixed regardless of changes in monetary policy and significant shifts in private demand, e.g., a plant-and-equipment boom. Apart from trying to correct such misconceptions, economists have had to wrestle with the problem of the overstatement of the full-employment surplus when inflation expands revenues faster than expenditures, not to mention the problem of weighting for differing multipliers if tax or expenditure components change sharply. In brief, the advances over the bad old days of the annually balanced budget objective are enormous, but economists are aware of the limitations of the full-employment-surplus measure and are struggling to resolve them.

Just as economics relegated erroneous budget concepts to the dustbin, so it has cast a shadow over such former favorites (of mine, among others) as federal capital budgeting and the "shelf of public works." The initial enthusiasm for the capital budget concept (in the context of a Congress seeking to balance the budget annually) was dispelled by second-thoughts analysis showing that (a) it rested on some faulty parallels with private finance, (b) the implicit fiscal policy rule of always financing capital projects by borrowing is in error, and (c) it would bias government capital spending toward bricks and mortar instead of brainpower and people. In the public works case, the concept ran afoul the findings of prosaic economic research: recent studies show that the public works program launched in 1963 to speed recovery was still not completed before excess demand overtook us in the 1966–69 period. This is not to rule out the use of certain types of "public works" that are nimble on their feet, such as road and forest maintenance work, for stabilization purposes. Nor does it rule out speeding up or delaying the launching of projects that are to be undertaken for sound cost-benefit reasons in any event. But it is fair warning not to expect very much stabilization help from the public works sector (not to be confused with public service employment).

In the conscious use of taxes for stabilization purposes, the huge 1964 income tax cut delivered economic expansion and a balanced budget on schedule without inflation by mid-1965, just before the Vietnam escalation struck the economy. The temporary 1968 surtax, buffeted by powerful demand forces and monetary easing, left a more ambiguous econometric trail. Subsequent fiscal policy thinking emphasizes the advantages of temporary tax changes that embody not just income effects but intertemporal substitution effects. For example, lowering the prices of investment goods in a recession via a clearly temporary increase in the investment credit, or temporary cuts in consumption taxes on durable goods (or lacking these, temporary purchase subsidies), would constitute a powerful incentive to purchase those goods before the price went up again.

Further work is needed to measure the cost-push effects of anti-inflationary tax increases that offset part of their demand-damping effect. In recession, the cost-easing and demand-push effects work in happy harmony. They work at cross purposes in tax increases (though not in expenditure cuts) to curb inflation. The question of how large the offsetting cost-push effects, or aggregate supply effects, may be is unresolved. In a high-inflation economy, this is a serious gap in our fiscal policy knowledge.

OTHER ASPECTS

This kaleidoscope of contributions, long as it is, leaves out a whole string of developments in budget concepts, techniques, and process—efforts that were crowned by the congressional budget reforms recently put into effect.

Much of the guidance and momentum for these reforms was provided by economic analysis and by a succession of five economists who served as budget directors throughout the 1960's. Also omitted is the conceptual work on the economics of the bureaucratic process, of how government works. Other omissions include the rebirth of interest and great advances in the economics of state and local finance, the rapid growth of the important new field of urban economics—with its contributions to regional economics, location research, and analysis of the city as an economic system—and the enriched economics of fiscal federalism. I have even eschewed an assessment of revenue sharing, the rationale and form of which were developed by economists. With little imperialism, economists can also cite the firm quantitative evidence being developed to demonstrate the adverse economic effects of many public regulatory activities.*

For all the advances, the agenda of unresolved conceptual questions and unfinished empirical business is huge. But even this truncated review of progress and current output in public economics makes clear that the contributions of recent decades have enormously enriched this field not only conceptually but as a source of hard practical advice to decision-makers who want to shape a better tax system, do justice to the poor, improve social programs, reform budget procedures, fight unemployment, and so on. And in the process, the frontiers of normative economics, both theoretical and empirical, have been pushed out into the areas of education, health, racism, crime, family behavior, and even political behavior.

As a result, we have plunged ever deeper into the realm of values. Not that it was a value-free inquiry to ask the traditional questions about the effect of a given policy on material output. But surely the testing of policies by the costs they incur and how effective they are in meeting some generally accepted criteria of social welfare or general welfare involves economics directly in value and distributional problems. And it enables economics to say important things on social policy issues within the framework of the conventional economic paradigm and with rigor of the nonmortis variety.

We are becoming interdisciplinary in spite of ourselves. When *we* do it, of course, we don't think of it as cross-sterilization of disciplines. But here is an area where modesty becomes us. For if we confine ourselves too narrowly to economics, we are far too likely to attribute to economic variables the behavior and results that are really a re-

---

* As an example of the "Age of Quantification," George Stigler cites the sea of studies on regulatory practices and their costs and benefits in the past dozen years, where there was a vacuum before. He notes that thirty-six "quantitative studies of effects of laws" were reported in two journals alone during this period, the *Journal of Law and Economics* and the *Journal of Political Economy.* These are promoting a broader consensus within the profession, informing decision-makers, and posing challenges that will make policy failures easier to identify. (Personal correspondence.)

sponse to social variables. Fearing just that, one observer has been unkind enough to suggest that we ought to stick to inflation problems where we *all* know what to say.

V. The Economist and Inflation

Inflation may no longer be "Public Enemy Number One" now that severe recession is upon us, but it is surely "Economists' Enemy Number One." Among the charges of, by, and against economists that have been touched off by double-digit inflation and reported in public print are these:

- Economists have confessed (I plead guilty) that 1973 was "the year of infamy in inflation forecasting" and, as already noted, that "we were caught with our parameters down."
- Aaron Gordon puts it more explicitly when he says that "the forecasters fell flat on their faces in predicting price changes because they didn't have any way of estimating sectoral supply scarcity" and adds that we have not "even started to develop a theory of aggregate supply."
- Wassily Leontief scolds macroeconomists more generally: "There is a lot of fancy methodology, but the macroeconomists get indigestion if you give them facts."
- We are reminded *ad nauseam* that the "new economists" of the 1960's had promised to fine-tune inflation out of their full-employment economy (a clearcut triumph of caricature over fact since Keynesians time and again warned of precisely the opposite danger).
- Gunnar Myrdal and Robert Heilbroner have pointed to stagflation as Exhibit A that economists typically lag rather than lead their targets, that being "behind its time" is "the regular methodological weakness of establishment economics."
- Friedrich Von Hayek recently reentered the fray to lay the blame for worldwide inflation squarely at the door of

economists, particularly those "who have embraced the teachings of Lord Keynes."

Apart from the charge that Keynesian economists have *caused* inflation (which is much like saying that the cause of forest fires is trees), the bill of particulars against macroeconomics runs something like this: First, economists did not forewarn the body politic that it would have to pay such a high price in endemic inflation for the attainment of high employment. Second, progress in solving some important puzzles of endemic inflation relating, for example, to the Phillips Curve, wage inflation, expectations, and uncertainty is much too slow. Third, there is no articulated general theory of inflation as such. Fourth, economists failed to foresee the 1973–74 epidemic inflation because their forecasting models lacked the central supply and price parameters. Fifth, macroeconomics is helpless in the face of epidemic or external-shock inflation—indeed, it has not satisfactorily explained the coexistence of inflation and recession, or stagflation. Without attempting a point-by-point assessment of these complaints, I will touch on all of them in the following sympathetic interpretation of how economists are coping with inflation's tough analytic and empirical challenges.

THE INFLATION-PRONE ECONOMY

Addressing myself for a moment to our reproachful public, let me simply say: "We never promised you a rose garden without thorns." Over most of the past thirty years, macroeconomists have warned again and again, first, that aggressive fiscal and monetary policy to manage aggregate demand was bound to generate inflationary pressures once the economy entered the full-employment zone, and second, that while full employment spells inflation, recessions run into price and wage rigidities that thwart deflation, an asymmetry bound to produce a ratchet effect on the price level. Keynes himself foresaw the basic problem in his little book *How to Pay for the War* in 1940. Abba Lerner and William Beveridge also wrote of the problem in the early 1940's. And it has been discussed in the stabilization theory and policy literature, in congressional hearings, and in other policy forums ever since.

This country finally embraced activist fiscal policies for full employment in the 1960's, most explicitly in the 1964 tax cut. Following the canons of Keynesian economics, focusing on the economy's full-employment potential as their target, and steadfastly rejecting a spate of "structural" explanations of unemployment, economists were at first alone in prescribing tax cuts as a tonic for the stagnant economy. Enacted early in 1964, the tax cut delivered the promised expansion and budget balance without inflation. By August 1965, when Vietnam escalation began, unemployment had been brought to 4.4 percent with only the faintest stirring of the inflationary beast (i.e., with consumer prices rising at less than a 2 percent annual rate).

In a very real sense, economists have been victims of their own success. Macroeconomic policy, capped by the tax cut, was the major force holding the postwar economy on a vastly higher plane than the prewar economy.* On one hand, the high-employment, limited-recession economy forged with our macroeconomic policy tools is indeed an inflation-prone economy—the formula for successful management of high-pressure prosperity is far more elusive than the formula for getting there. Yet, on the other, success bred great expectations on the part of the public that economics could deliver prosperity without inflation and with ever-growing material gains in the bargain. The message got through that we had "harnessed the existing

---

* As gauges of the contrast between prewar and postwar performance: unemployment averaged 18.8 percent in the decade of depression (1931–40) in contrast with 4.8 percent in the twenty-eight years since World War II; the prewar peak annual rate was 24.9 percent, the postwar peak was 6.8 percent. Annual real GNP dropped 30 percent from 1929 to 1933; since the war, mild declines have occurred only in three years (1949, 1954, and 1970), though 1974–75 may add two more. Consumer prices in 1940 were 18 percent below 1929; from 1948 to 1974, they increased 106 percent.

economics . . . to the purposes of prosperity, stability, and growth," and that as to the role of the tax cut in breaking old molds of thinking, "Nothing succeeds like success" (Heller [1966]). *The Economist* unkindly corrected me: "Nothing *exceeds* like success."*

To be sure, critics and converts alike ignored our caveats that the goal of "prosperity without a price-wage spiral" had "eluded not only this country but all of its industrial partners in the free world," that "the margin for error diminishes as the economy reaches the treasured but treacherous area of full employment . . . ," and that "the 'new economics' promises no money-back guarantees against occasional slowdowns or even recessions" (Heller [1966].

All too soon, Vietnam blew the economy off course. Economists found that in the political arena fiscal policy was not a two-way street and that the much delayed surtax adopted in mid-1968 was no match for surging inflation. Nor was the induced recession of 1969–70. It took a combination of the 1971 shock therapy of tight wage-price controls and the stimulus of tax cuts to subdue inflation and energize expansion. It is worth noting that economists analyzed and projected the effects of this "new economic policy" with exceptional precision. That the tax cuts, coupled with controls and devaluation, would generate a surging expansion at very moderate rates of inflation in 1972 was widely and accurately forecast.

But the period from August 1971 to January 1973 was in the nature of a remission from the inflationary disease, clearly not a cure. The 1969–70 recession brought home the worsening problem of persistent inflation in the face of

---

* Macroeconomists were not alone in their exuberance in the mid-1960's. A decade ago, George Stigler, after reviewing the great promises and early accomplishments of the "Quantitative Revolution in Economics," was moved to say, "I am convinced that economics is finally at the threshold of its Golden Age—nay, we already have one foot through the door. . . . Our expanding theoretical and empirical studies will inevitably and irresistibly enter into the subject of public policy, and we shall develop a body of knowledge essential to intelligent policy formulation. And then, quite frankly, I hope that we become the ornaments of democratic society whose opinions on economic policy shall prevail."

slowdown and recession. It presented new empirical puzzles for the analysts of the Phillips Curve, wage equations, and expectational inflation. And it began to prompt the public muttering that was later intensified by the 1974–75 stagflation: "All right, so you didn't promise us a rose garden without thorns—but the thorns without the rose garden?"

Keenly aware of these problems, economists have long been at the drawing boards on this problem of endemic inflation. In a close parallel with research on cancer, economists are working on various pieces of the inflation puzzle and producing useful insights and guidance for policy purposes. But as economists, we would be the first to underscore that these puzzles are far from being fitted into an articulated and holistic theory of inflation. Inflationary analysis appears as an appendage to Keynesian and monetarist theories. But as yet, the Keynesian apparatus cannot tell us how any given change in aggregate demand is divided between changes in real output and changes in prices. Nor has monetarist theory unlocked the puzzle of how the effects of monetary changes are divided between output and price level changes. And no big breakthrough is in sight.

THE 1973–74 EPIDEMIC

Does this mean that the economist has to stand mute in the meanwhile? Not at all. He is pushing ahead on the various pieces of basic research on the cancer of inflation and isolating and prescribing effectively for particular forms of the cancer even without having a complete explanation of the disease. Let me come back to the sustained and systematic research efforts on endemic inflation after examining the 1973–74 epidemic and the economist's responses to it. Since the epidemic is an over-layer on the endemic base, the distinctions won't be clear-cut—but they are nonetheless useful for viewing what the economist is able to contribute to policy.

The food-fuel price bulge generated over half of the 1973–74 inflation—and of economists' woes as well. Yet it is asking a lot of economists to expect them to have foreseen that the oil cartel would quadruple oil prices, that the world would suffer widespread and successive crop failures, that the Peruvian anchovies would go into hiding, and that the Soviets would "solve our surplus grain problem" overnight.

Several unpleasant policy surprises also beset the inflation forecasters. First, just when a new rash of inflation was breaking out early in 1973, the reasonably effective Phase II controls were abruptly dropped in favor of the weak and ineffective Phase III. Second, six months later, after inflation had changed into a commodity-driven structural phenomenon involving a drastic readjustment of relative prices, the White House (to the pained surprise of economists inside and outside the Administration) prescribed just the wrong medicine, a new wage-price freeze. A third policy surprise was that the dollar was allowed to sink like a stone: At its low point in the summer of 1973 (just before a substantial rebound), relative prices of imports had risen 10 percent in six months. About a quarter of the 1973 inflation has been attributed to these policy developments. (Nordhaus and Shoven [1974]).

It is worth noting that unexpected twists and turns of federal policy—which might be termed "internal shocks" in contrast with the "external shocks" of the food-fuel price explosion—are a continuing bane of the forecaster's existence. The about-face of the Federal Reserve in 1974 is another painful case in point. The sharp turn from ease to tightness in the first quarter of the year was a major factor in transforming prospects of recovery into recession in the second half of 1974. It is not quite clear why economists should be better at anticipating these shocks, especially the external ones, than society as a whole, or other professional specialists, or practical men of the world. Nothing in statistical methodology or economic science enables us to predict random shocks. What *can* be expected of us is that when they occur, we will spot them quickly, identify them, and analyze their significance for policy.

It is also worth remembering that democratic governments, by their nature, are pressure-responders rather than problem-anticipators. This carries two implications for political economists. On one hand, if an idea's time has not yet come, or if a problem has not yet become a crisis, the economist's call for action is likely to go unheeded. On the other, spotting emergent problems early can perhaps hasten an idea's time and alert the policy makers to impending danger.

Economists can more readily be faulted for being caught by surprise, first, by the shortages of materials and primary processing capacity that caused the economy to bump against its ceiling sooner than expected and, second, by the worldwide economic boom that put severe pressure on raw commodity supplies and prices. On the first point, we suffered both from information failure—the official capacity indexes simply did not reveal how close the economy was to its output ceilings—and from analytic limits. While identifying the causes, economists have been unable to pinpoint the relative significance of the shortfall of investment that began in the late 1960's, of underinvestment caused by price controls, of delays induced by environmental policies, and of the surge of foreign demand touched off by devaluation. However, I should add that the shortages problem is meat and drink for economists, and they are responding (especially in the energy field) with new analyses of price elasticities, investment needs, and the like. All of a sudden, price theory is back in vogue, and elasticities have replaced multipliers as the badge of a policymaker's *savoir faire*.

Delays in perceiving that the U.S. economic expansion was part of a worldwide upsurge can again be laid more to lack of an adequate information system than to any inability to understand the underlying principles. Still, a better sense of history and of the emerging worldwide imbalance between growing aspirations and growing incomes on one hand and inelastic resource supply and lagging technology on the other would have made us more conscious and cautious. We are less likely to be caught by surprise in the future in view of the new worldwide data networks that are being developed by Project LINK at the University of Pennsylvania and by Otto Eckstein and his colleagues at Data Resources Incorporated (DRI).

Without absolving economists, one should apply this operational test: With proper foresight, would tighter monetary and budget policy have been able to damp inflation? It is worth recalling, first, that the full-employment budget was making a swing of over $10 billion toward restraint between fiscal 1973 and fiscal 1974 (from a $2 billion deficit to a $10 billion surplus under the old 4 percent unemployment standard) and that monetary policy pushed interest rates into the double-digit region; second, that there was little that an aggregate demand squeeze could have done to push world commodity prices down. So the answer is clear: Even tougher fiscal and monetary policy would have had limited scope in holding inflation down.

This is not to deny that generating a larger full-employment surplus would have been the prudent course in calendar 1973. But it is worth noting that to offset the food and fuel price explosions—which were triggered by forces largely immune to U.S. fiscal and monetary policy— would have required a reduction of 3 percent in all other prices. Such a target implies depression-inducing doses of fiscal and monetary restriction, an unthinkable "solution."

Looking toward the future, many economists draw the lesson not that one should keep the economy's motor idling, but rather that one should provide it with safety devices and heavy-duty shock absorbers, for example, stockpiling of foodstuffs, oil, and basic raw materials, careful tracking of commodity exports, distant early warning systems to spot shortages-in-the-making, and conservation and development measures to limit dependence on foreign raw materials cartels. In other words, it is a call for better planning, better data, and faster conversion of knowledge into policy.

Another criterion of economists' responses to inflationary shocks is how quickly they adapted (read, "disag-
gregated") their macro-models, large and small, to incorporate new supply and price parameters that had previously
been judged of second or third order importance and
hence relegated to Alfred Marshall's *ceteris paribus*
pound. Some of the mongrel pups impounded there turned
out to be full-blooded huskies, for example, food prices, the
exchange value of the dollar, oil and other raw material
supplies and prices. At first, economists were slow, and the
big models were sluggish, in their responses. After all, for
two decades prices had moved in tandem with wages, with
a year-by-year percentage-point differential of $2\frac{3}{4} \pm 1$. So
most models relied on wage trends, with some adjustment
for productivity and capacity behavior, to give them a fix
on price trends. Their eyes were on labor market indicators
rather than commodity supplies, exchange rates, and the
like.

After some initial delays, the model builders scrambled
to disaggregate, to build micro-elements into their macro-
models. For example, DRI now has good stage-of-process-
ing models that absorb the impacts of food and energy
price explosions. Price elasticities are being built into the
macro-models to reflect the impact of massive relative
price changes on the macro-dimensions of the economy.

The whole experience reminds us of the role and limits
of econometric forecasting models. First, the combination
of computers, mathematics, and econometrics cannot produce the miracles that the uninitiated may expect of
them—there is no way of replicating reality with its three
million equations, all of them nonlinear. Second, their in-
dispensable function is to bring us closer to reality and
help the mind manage the previously unmanageable—
they permit us to release vastly more animals from the *ceteris paribus* pound than we could manage without these
tools. Third, they have to be constantly adjusted to plug in
common sense, adjust the length of the lags, and bring in

new dimensions of the problem. Else, they will lock out things that a more judgmental approach would include and will fail to respond quickly to changes in order of importance.

So the inflation-shock experience has brought home the need not just to watch supply but to watch *all* the pieces lest the model prevail over the mind, rather than having the model help the mind prevail over matter. The macro-stalactites have to reach toward the micro-stalagmites, and vice-versa. I hope that metaphor is not a portent of the pace at which the advance toward macro-micro fusion will proceed.

A case in point was the early analysis, especially by George Perry, of the macro-impact of the oil price increase. By late 1973, his work had already highlighted the oil paradox—the *in*flation of costs and hence prices, leading to a *de*flation of aggregate demand—and had provided some estimates of both. His finding that some $15 to $20 billion of consumer purchasing power would be siphoned off into the hands of oil producers and royalty collectors without any early return to the economy in the form of demand for imports or investment goods had important implications for demand-management policy—implications that were ignored until severe recession was full upon us.*

These important insights into the macroeconomic policy implications of oil prices fit into the broader efforts of economists to disentangle the sources of the current inflation and identify the appropriate remedies. They differentiate among (1) excess demand, which had spent most of its force by early 1974, (2) the price-wage-price spiral, which

---

*Late in 1974, Perry undertook a more searching econometric probe with the benefit of actual rather than projected oil price data and with the aid of the large-scale formal models. His analysis shows that the purchasing power loss had reached $37 billion by the third quarter of 1974 and that the rise in the deflator attributable to the oil price jump was 3.8 percent. His analysis embraced not only the real-income effect (the transfer of real income from consumers to producers), but also the monetary-policy effect (the reduction of the real value of the money stock and the rise in interest rates stemming from the highly inelastic short-run demand for petroleum products), the automobile-demand effect (higher saving) and the induced-inflation effect (the price-wage-price effect) of the oil price rise on the macroeconomy.

began to turn more rapidly in 1974, and (3) external-shock or special-sector inflation, in particular the commodity-price surges that permeate the present inflation and account for its special character and ferocity.

The first responds rather readily to monetary-fiscal pressure, the second responds more reluctantly, and the third is highly resistant to the demand-management measures of any given country. For the second and especially the third types, therefore, high costs in unemployment and foregone output have to be incurred for small gains in curbing inflation. So the distinction is an instructive one for policy—even when the instructions are ignored. Now the economic lessons that were so long ignored are being painfully driven home by severe recession and unemployment coupled with continuing inflation. A much-belated consensus that fiscal stimulus can be undertaken with minimal inflationary risk is rapidly forming.

The economists' three-ply classification of inflation sources is also useful in driving home another point: In most U.S. inflations, consisting of the first two types, one person's price is another person's income, so that in spite of some reshuffling, there is no net loss in real income. Not so in 1973–75. Commodity inflation has transferred tens of billions of dollars of *real* income out of the pockets of urban consumers and wage earners into the hands of farmers and foreigners, where it is beyond the reach of the collective bargaining process. From this, several important inferences can be drawn:

- Point for point, this inflation *cum* relative price changes is harsher in its impact than previous post war inflations.
- In this "no-win" inflation, the wage earner's loss has not generally been the employer's gain; hence, if the wage "catch-up" process succeeds in recouping the *full* rise in the cost of living, much of the wage increase will pass through to prices and thereby give the wage-price spiral another self-defeating turn.

- It follows, as various economists urged throughout 1974, that tax cuts to bolster the real income of labor, if put in the context of a social contract, might well relieve some of the pressure for higher wages.

In this respect, today's situation contrasts rather sharply with the 1950–51 inflation, when a similarly rapid runup in world commodity prices was accompanied by a rapid rise in profit margins side-by-side with vigorous federal policies to boost capacity. The ensuing combination of ebbing world market prices and wage increases that could be granted without generating higher product prices resulted in a remarkable four-year period of price stability from 1952 to 1956.

A closely allied economic insight goes to the nature of the inflationary process. It explains in good part, first, why inflation is so stubborn even in the face of overly restrictive monetary-fiscal policy and rapidly mounting unemployment and slack in the economy. It is the sharp runup in *relative* prices of food, fuel, and imported goods—coupled with the downward rigidities of wages and prices—that is the key to most of our stagflationary malaise today.

These downward rigidities are a striking example of the way in which economic solutions create their own problems and move the economist relentlessly from one new frontier to another. Once macroeconomics gave governments the know-how and tools of modern demand-management to avoid depression, and once the public caught on that even recessions are essentially manmade—chiefly by That Man in the White House, whoever he is, together with the Congress and the Federal Reserve Board—it became part of the politics of survival to hold employment high and keep recessions in check. Absent the fears of mass unemployment and prolonged recession, the risks of not cutting prices and not accepting lower wages are minimized. Having put the Great Depression of the 1930's far behind us, will we therefore have to live with Great Inflation of the 1970's?

Essentially, the economist answers that, given the ratchet behavior of wages and prices, the price level can only float upward to accommodate the huge relative price increases of oil, grains, certain raw materials, and imported goods. These sharp changes in the composition of supply touch off reverberating price increases throughout the economy as prices in the scarce-supply sectors become costs in the less-scarce ones. The reverberations go on—in substantial part independent of the state of aggregate demand and hence of monetary and fiscal policy—until the prices of the initiating goods have risen sufficiently farther than prices in general to accomplish the necessary realignment of relative prices. This is the process going on now. It takes time, but not forever. It has much to do with double-digit inflation, but it does not condemn us to Weimar Republic inflation.

Solow (1975) reminds us that the supply-shift phenomenon bears a close relationship to the demand-shift analysis of the creeping inflation of the mid-1950's. At that time, the parallel process was touched off by an investment boom that put excess demand pressures on capital goods industries even when there was no excess aggregate demand in the economy. Given the downward rigidity and cost-oriented nature of wages and prices in areas of excess market power, the price level had to float upward to accommodate those relative price changes (Schultze [1959]).

John Dunlop and other economists have emphasized that there is a closely related phenomenon on the wage side known as "scale wages" or "wage relativities" or even a "just wage" (Hall [1974] and Piore [1974]). If the relative wage scale is thrown out of kilter by an outsized settlement in one industry, the others will writhe, twist, and turn until the old relationships are reestablished. There is only one way the wage structure can move to accommodate this process: up. Again, the process burns itself out only when a new equilibrium has been established on a higher plateau.

The policy implications of the supply-shift, demand-shift, and wage-shift insights are reasonably clear. One is the limited scope of repressive monetary-fiscal policy in coping with this process. Another is that the key to a successful wage-price policy for these circumstances is to establish and effectuate norms for the pace-setters and thus thwart the wage-wage and price-price spirals and the interacting wage-price spiral. Once the process is launched, the role of a wage-price watchdog with teeth would be to see to it that the adjustment process is a limited and straightforward one, not a leapfrogging sequence that will prolong the agony of adjustment. Again, understanding the economics of the process is the *sine qua non* for shaping the right policy to fit the particular type and phase of inflation that is beleaguering us.

An intriguing and productive effort to provide a better understanding of economic processes and relationships that bear on economic policy decisions has been undertaken by the Brookings Panel on Economic Activity. It seeks to focus the best analytical and empirical weapons economics can offer on such policy problems and puzzles as the Phillips Curve relationship and wage equations, the economy's reaction to external inflationary shocks, the impact of wage-price controls, measurement of capacity utilization, the cost of unemployment, and the impacts of monetary and fiscal policy. In the course of examining these issues and bringing academic work into closer contact with firing-line policy problems, the Brookings Panel conducts an exercise in what one might call "continuing confrontational econometrics." Mindful of the pitfalls cited earlier in this paper, the Panel combines rigorous quantitative testing with continuing surveillance by one's peers to assure that the investigator (a) looks beyond mathematics and makes his assumptions and relations conform to common sense, (b) spells out the implications of his econometrics and, if they are implausible, tries again, and (c) constantly keeps asking questions of the model. With the Panel now going into its sixth year of thrice-yearly meetings and publications (*Brookings Papers on Economic Activity*), previous analyses become, not undisturbed museum pieces, but grist for the mill of constant retesting under the harsh light of reality and peer-group criticism.

SOME PROBLEMS OF ENDEMIC INFLATION

Let me return briefly to some of the abiding problems of endemic inflation that are engaging the attention and efforts of economists.

An important but elusive question for the policy maker concerns the costs of inflation. Can the economist tell him or her anything useful and definitive on this subject? Useful, perhaps. Definitive, no. First, the economist would remind him that people continually blame inflation for crimes it does not commit. They are sure that every increase in their pay envelope is a reward for merit, every increase in prices an inflationary theft. Especially pertinent to our present shock-spiral is the observation that people "blame inflation for changes in relative prices and in real incomes that stem from market forces that have nothing to do with the course of the general price level." (Foster [1972])

Second, studies show that in a typical U.S. inflation, the poor have gained more in jobs and incomes than they have lost in higher prices. But in the present inflation, prices have shifted sharply against the poor and any initial gains they may have made in jobs and income in 1973 have been more than offset by the losses incurred in the deepening 1974–75 recession induced to fight inflation.

Third, at the rates of inflation experienced prior to the 1973–75 explosion, most economists find it difficult to believe that the costs of inflation—mostly in redistributional effects, but with some distortion in resource allocation—hold a candle to the welfare losses of substantial add-ons to unemployment. Fourth, however, when inflation rates reach double-digit levels, the costs in terms of the social conflicts and tensions it generates and the uncertainties and loss of confidence in the dollar yardstick it may breed are important intangibles that economists cannot ignore, yet have not been able to quantify. We need to understand far more about what unsettles and upsets people about inflation, how this affects their economic behavior, and what economic costs result. Clearly, in an economy where inflation is endemic, the balance between its gains and losses deserves intensive further study.

Another important question is this: How much of the present runup in prices of foodstuffs, oil, and raw materials is a transitory phenomenon, how much is a one-time shift to a new plateau, and how much represents a new upward trend? Economists have trained their guns of price theory and price elasticity estimation on these questions. For oil and several other basic materials in short supply, they generally come up with more optimistic answers for five to ten years hence than for the near term. But much of the answer depends on geopolitical, meteorological, and similar puzzles—for example, the effectiveness of oil and other raw material cartels, the pace of world population increases and income growth, and the possibility of a dry, cold phase in world weather—that lie largely or wholly beyond the reach of economic analysis.

What we do know is this: The 1950's and the 1960's were a period of gently declining or roughly stable world prices for raw materials and foodstuffs. Now rising population, industrialization, income, and aspirations may put such pressure on the world's supply capabilities that— while we are not near any Club-of-Rome ultimate limits— we may for some time exceed the speed limits of stable expansion. If so, we may have passed an inflection point in the price trends of basic inputs to the economy. (Rostow, [1974]) The mild downward trend of the 1951–71 period facilitated the rise in real incomes of urban workers side-by-side with rising profits. If this trend is reversed, rising income claims will generate greater strains, and the Phillips Curve trade-off will take place around a higher inflation constant. Economic analyses of long-run supply prices of basic commodities using alternative assumptions regarding world political, weather, and economic trends might be a useful aid to rational economic planning.

Coming back into the domain of economics as such, one should take account of the important new thinking and efforts now being devoted to the continuing mysteries of industrial pricing policies and the role of fixed-rule (generally, mark-up) pricing as a shield against uncertainty. Answering the question of how, and how fast, supply-shifts in the auction markets or market-oriented sector are transmitted through the rule-determined sector—where certain relativities seem to be maintained in the structure of prices (and wages)—is essential to an understanding of structural inflation (Piore [1974]).

In turn, this analysis will strongly influence thinking on government intervention in private wage-price and perhaps also supply-demand decisions. If the wage-price structure is indeed fairly rigid and if supply- and demand-shifts set off an inflationary spiral, the "natural market forces" will not readily make the necessary supply-demand adjustment in any case. Wage-price restraints or controls would not be supplanting some supple and efficient resource allocation mechanism, yet would insert a circuit-breaker into the inflationary spiral. This view of the world would also suggest that government action to stimulate supply and suppress demand at certain pressure points in the economy might well pass the test of economic efficiency. In pursuing these questions and hypotheses, the economist will be laying a firmer conceptual and empirical foundation for specifying the areas and circumstances in which intervention may be the lesser evil.

CONCLUSION

I have dealt at some length with the substance of economists' work and findings on inflation because mere assertions of progress would hardly suffice to demonstrate what's right with economics in this most vulnerable area.

The fact that there are no final or comprehensive answers has not kept economists from making significant distinctions, analyses, and measurements that equip policy makers with better means of judging the policy trade-offs and determining how to improve the fit of policy-to-problem for the different types and stages of inflation. When policy makers fail to heed these lessons, as in 1974, both the economy and the economist feel the backlash.

Throughout this discourse, I have time and again been tempted to kick over the traces I fastened on myself and give voice to my own criticisms, dissatisfactions, and admonitions. But since an unholy (and unwitting) alliance of my colleagues and outside critics has amply and ably taken care of this, I felt it best to stay within my constraints in the interest of doing what I could to redress the balance. As economists, we have many sins, none deadly, to confess. But these are far outweighed by the virtues, all quite lively, that we can legitimately profess.

References

Henry Aaron, "A New View of Property Tax Incidence," *American Economic Review Proceedings*, May 1974, 54, 2, 212–21.

Barbara R. Bergmann, "Economist, Poll Thy People," *New York Times* "Points of View," November 3, 1974.

William H. Beveridge, *Full-Employment in a Free Society*, London, 1944.

James H. Blackman, "The Outlook for Economics," *Southern Economic Journal*, April 1971, 37, 385–95.

Alan S. Blinder and Robert M. Solow, *et al*, "Analytical Foundations of Fiscal Policy," *Economics of Public Finance*, Brookings Institution, Washington, D.C., 1974, 3–118.

Kenneth Boulding, "Economics as a Moral Science," *American Economic Review*, March 1969, 59, 1, 1–12.

Howard R. Bowen, "Toward a Humanist Economics," *Nebraska Journal of Economics and Business*, Autumn 1972, 11, 4, 9–24.

Edward Foster, "Costs and Benefits of Inflation," Federal Reserve Bank of Minneapolis, March, 1972.

John K. Galbraith, "Power and the Useful Economist," *American Economic Review*, March 1973, 58, 1–11.

F. H. Hahn, "Some Adjustment Problems," *Econometrica*, January 1970, 38, 1–17.

Robert E. Hall, "The Process of Inflation in the Labor Market," *Brookings Papers on Economic Activity*, Brookings Institution, Washington, D.C., 1974, 2, 343–410.

Robert L. Heilbroner, "Economics as a 'Value-Free' Science," *Social Research*, Spring 1973, 40, 129–43.

Walter W. Heller, *New Dimensions of Political Economy*, Cambridge, 1966.

Harry G. Johnson, "The Economic Approach to Social Questions," *Economica*, February 1968, 35, 1–21.

———, "Scholars as Public Adversaries: The Case of Economics," in Charles Frankel, ed., *Controversies and Decisions: The Social Sciences and Public Policy*, Russell Sage Foundation, New York, 1976.

John Maynard Keynes, *How to Pay for the War*, London, 1940.

Wassily Leontief, "Theoretical Assumptions and Non-observed Facts," *American Economic Review*, March 1971, 61, 1–7.

Abba P. Lerner, "Functional Finance and the Federal Debt," *Social Research*, February 1943, 10, 38–51.

Donald MacDougall, "In Praise of Economics," *Economic Journal*, December 1974, 84, 773–86.

Sherman J. Maisel, "The Economics and Finance Literature and Decision Making," *The Journal of Finance*, May 1974, 29, 313–22.

Richard A. Musgrave, *The Theory of Public Finance*, New York, 1959.

Gunnar Myrdal, *Asian Drama: An Inquiry into the Poverty of Nations*, Vol I, New York, 1968.

William Nordhaus and John Shoven, "Inflation 1973: The Year of Infamy," *Challenge*, May–June 1974, 17, 14–22.

Arthur M. Okun, *The Political Economy of Prosperity*, Brookings Institution, Washington, D.C., 1969.

Joseph A. Pechman and Benjamin A. Okner, *Who Bears*

the Tax Burden? Brookings Institution, Washington, D.C., 1974.

George L. Perry, "The Petroleum Crisis and the U.S. Economy," in *Higher Oil Prices and the World Economy*, Brookings Institution, Washington, D.C., 1975.

E.H. Phelps Brown, "The Underdevelopment of Economics," *Economic Journal*, March 1972, 82, 1–10.

Michael Piore, "Curing Inflation With Unemployment, Outmoded Notions of Supply and Demand," *The New Republic*, November 2, 1974, 171, 27–31.

Alice M. Rivlin, *Systematic Thinking for Social Action*, Brookings Institution, Washington, D.C., 1971.

———, "Why Can't We Get Things Done?" *The Brookings Bulletin*, Spring 1972, 9, 5–9.

———, "Social Experiments: The Promise and the Problem," *Evaluation*, 1973, 1, 77–78.

Marc J. Roberts, "On the Nature and Condition of Social Science," *Daedalus*, Summer 1974, 103, 47–64.

Walt W. Rostow, "Political Economy in a Time of Scarcity: How to Get from Here to There," *Naval War College Review*, September–October 1974, 27, 32–45.

Nancy Ruggles, ed., *Economics*, Englewood Cliffs, New Jersey, 1970.

Paul A. Samuelson, "The Pure Theory of Public Expenditures," *Review of Economics and Statistics*, November 1954, pp. 387–89.

Charles L. Schultze, *Recent Inflation in the U.S.*, Joint Economic Committee, Working Paper #1, Congress of the United States, Washington D.C., 1959.

———, "The Reviewers Reviewed," *American Economic Review Proceedings*, May 1971, 51, 45–52.

———, "Is Economics Obsolete? No, Underemployed," *Saturday Review*, January 22, 1972, 55, 50–57.

Theodore W. Schultz, *et al*, "Human Capital: Policy Issues and Research Opportunities," *Human Resources*, National Bureau of Economic Research, New York, 1972.

Carl S. Shoup, *et al*, *Public Expenditures and Taxation*, National Bureau of Economic Research, New York, 1972.

Robert M. Solow, "Science and Ideology in Economics," *The Public Interest*, Fall 1970, 21, 94–107.

———, "The State of Economics—Discussion," *American Economic Review Proceedings*, May 1971, 51, 63–68.

———, "The Intelligent Citizen's Guide to Inflation," *The Public Interest*, Winter 1975, 38, 20–66.

George J. Stigler, "The Economist and the State," *American Economic Review*, March 1965, 55, 1–18.

Paul Sweezy, "Capitalism, for Worse," *Monthly Review*, February 1974, 25, 1–7.

James Tobin, "Cambridge (U.K. vs. Cambridge (Mass.)," *The Public Interest*, Spring 1973, 31, 102–9.

———, *The New Economics One Decade Older*, Princeton, 1974.

Frederick A. von Hayek, "Inflation and Unemployment," *New York Times* "Points of View," November 15, 1974.

Benjamin Ward, *What's Wrong with Economics?* New York, 1972.

G. D. N. Worswick, "Is Progress in Economic Science Possible?" *The Economic Journal*, March 1972, 82, 73–79.

Index

215